Rhetoric and the New Testament

Rhetoric and the New Testament

by
Burton L. Mack

FORTRESS PRESS
Minneapolis

RHETORIC AND THE NEW TESTAMENT

Library of Congress Cataloging-in-Publication Data

Mack, Burton L.
    Rhetoric and the New Testament / Burton L. Mack.
        p.   cm.—(Guides to biblical scholarship. New Testament
series)
    Bibliography: p.
    ISBN 0-8006-2395-9
    1. Rhetoric in the Bible.   2. Rhetorical criticism.   3. Bible.
N.T.—Language, style,   I. Title.   II. Series.
BS2370.M33   1990
225.6'6—dc20   89-36039
                                                                CIP

The paper used in this publication meets the minimum requirements of American National Standard for Information Sciences—Permanence of Paper for Printed Library Materials, ANSI Z329.48-1984.   ∞™

Manufactured in the U.S.A.   AF 1-2395

94   93   92   91   90   1   2   3   4   5   6   7   8   9   10

Contents

6

Editor's Foreword

This volume by Burton Mack continues the interest of the series in formal matters, drawing together as it does social-historical and literary issues. It proceeds from the basic insight of the new rhetoric—which is actually a rediscovery of the real intention of the old rhetoric—that rhetoric is not a matter of stylistic ornamentation but of a persuasive argumentation. The comprehensive scope of the book lays out the historical factors surrounding the loss and recovery of rhetorical understanding in dealing with the New Testament, describes classical Greco-Roman rhetoric, applies rhetorical categories to the interpretation of a selection of New Testament texts, and analyzes the place of rhetorical criticism in the configuration of critical methods and hermeneutics. Mack makes interesting observations about the historical probability of New Testament writers and even bearers of Palestinian traditions being influenced by Greco-Roman rhetorical theory and practice.

Professor Mack believes that rhetorical criticism should take its place as one critical method complementing the work of the others. It should be especially valuable as a mediator between literary-critical and social-historical analyses because it pays attention to both the formal shaping of the text and the impact of the life setting on the employment of literary devices and the structuring of the argument.

Dan O. Via
Duke Divinity School

Introduction:

The Challenge of Rhetorical Criticism

When Mark pictured Jesus first teaching in public, he explained that "he taught them . . . by parables" (Mark 4:2). Readers of Mark's time would have known about the rhetorical significance of a parable (*parabolē*, "analogy") and would have recognized that Mark made his point by depicting a very distinctive rhetoric for Jesus. When the community of Q imagined Jesus warning his followers about "speaking a word against" the Son of man (Luke 12:10), they used the technical terminology for making a speech of prosecution in a court of law. When Paul explained to the Corinthians that he did not preach the gospel "with eloquent wisdom, lest the cross of Christ be emptied of its power" (1 Cor. 1:17), he made the contrast by reference to a style of oratory familiar to his listeners. When the author of the Letter to the Hebrews wanted to emphasize the importance of paying attention to the message Christians had heard, he wrote, "It was declared at the first by the Lord, and it was attested to us by those who heard him, while God also bore witness . . ." (Heb. 2:1–4), thus making use of common rhetorical idiom even though the message was set forth as a divine persuasion.

It may at first seem surprising that New Testament authors described the novelty of early Christian speech in terms of contrast to conventional rhetorics. It may be even more surprising to discover further that New Testament authors nevertheless made abundant use of rhetorical figures and patterns of argumentation customary for their cultures of context. If so, the surprise is surely due to the demise, some time during the last century, of the long and illustrious tradition of rhetoric at the heart of Western education and culture. The surprise, to be frank, is on us. From the beginning it was not so.

From the beginning it was taken for granted that the writings produced by early Christians were to be read as rhetorical compositions. Origen, for example, or Augustine, knew no other school for making sense of written compositions but the school of rhetoric. One can follow the rhetorical reading of the New Testament through the Middle Ages and into the early period of the Reformation where, for instance, Martin Bucer and Heinrich Bollinger simply assumed that Paul should be read through the eyes of Quintilian. Then, for most of the period of critical scholarship as well, the rhetoric of New Testament writings was explored as a matter of course.

New Testament scholars of the last three centuries learned their rhetoric in the normal course of their education in the humanities. The standard curriculum can be traced through Western history right back to the Greco-Roman age where the study of rhetoric was firmly ensconced in the *trivium,* those literary and philosophical studies that formed the foundation for the seven liberal arts. The *trivium* consisted of grammar, dialectic, and rhetoric; the *quadrivium* of geometry, arithmetic, astronomy, and music. The textbooks for instruction in rhetoric were the classics: Priscian's Latin translation of Hermogenes' *Progymnasmata*, and the works of Quintilian. These and other classical texts of rhetoric were still being copied and used well into the period of the Enlightenment. For twentieth-century scholars unfamiliar with this history, George Kennedy has recounted the story in his *Classical Rhetoric and its Christian and Secular Tradition from Ancient to Modern Times.*

It was not only natural for scholars of the last three centuries to read New Testament texts rhetorically, it was also necessary that they did. Manuscripts had to be collected and assessed, critical texts reconstructed, and scholarly apparatus prepared. This meant that the ancient languages had to be mastered and that matters of philology (the meaning of words), grammar, syntax, figurative language, tropes, idioms, and stylistic variations all had to be checked against classical authors and conventions. Knowledge of Greek grammar and rhetoric was absolutely essential to the fundamental task of establishing a text and rendering a translation. Rhetorical considerations were therefore part and parcel of the enormous labor these scholars expended in the production of lexica, grammars, and commentaries for the study of biblical texts.

Scholars working with *A Greek Grammar of the New Testament* by Blass, Debrunner, and Funk will recognize the importance of rhetorical observations when working out the syntax and translation for a New Testament text. The very descriptions of syntactical matters are replete with rhetorical designations and terms. One encounters, for instance, terms such as *anacoluthon, antithesis, ellipsis, paronomasia, periphrasis,* and many other terms for figures, stylistic traits, and ways of putting words together that have rhetorical significance. These identifications are a legacy to us of the Western rhetorical tradition.

And when the modern scholar turns to the standard *Greek-English Lexicon* by Liddell and Scott, a monumental labor first published in 1843 and now in its ninth edition, a reference to classical rhetoric will regularly be found for a host of common terms that were also used technically in that field of discourse. New Testament scholars alert to this phenomenon may be aware of the frequency with which many of these terms occur in early Christian usage, as well as with the fact that their rhetorical connotation is easily lost in modern translations.

With the rise of biblical scholarship as a discipline during the late seventeenth and eighteenth centuries, monographs and special studies began to appear that specifically addressed the question of the rhetoric of New Testament texts. One milestone can be identified in two eighteenth-century works by Karl Ludwig Bauer, one on Paul's manner of argumentation and the other on his employment of classical rhetorical techniques (1774, 1782). Another monument is a work by Christian Wilke, who emphasized the peculiar features of early Christian rhetoric when compared with classical patterns (1843). Toward the end of the nineteenth century an amazing accumulation of rhetorical detail was available to the scholar of the New Testament. Carl Heinrici's commentary on 2 Corinthians (1887), for instance, is a fine example of appeal to classical parallels for the elucidation of the rhetoric of the text. It stands in a tradition of scholarly commentaries that can be traced through the works of Johannes Weiss and the commentary on 2 Corinthians by Hans Wendland (1924) to the recent commentaries on Galatians and 2 Corinthians 8 and 9 by Hans-Dieter Betz (1979, 1985).

The commentaries by Betz illustrate the tenuous link to the past characteristic of the modern practice of rhetorical criticism. Because they stand in the tradition of German rhetorical commentaries, they serve to remind us of that illustrious history and to suggest that the knowledge of rhetoric won by that intellectual labor was not completely lost to the tradition of biblical scholarship. Nevertheless, they also have been hailed by most reviewers as a harbinger of the current rediscovery of rhetoric among biblical scholars, thus serving to remind us that the knowledge of rhetoric actually was lost to us in the twists and turns of twentieth-century scholarship. We now know that interest in rhetoric waned around the turn of the century, ushering in approximately four generations of scholarship without formal training in rhetoric and with very little knowledge of the tradition of rhetorical criticism. Betz's commentaries took biblical scholars by surprise because biblical scholarship had lost its rhetorical bearings.

Modern scholars are not to be faulted for their lack of firsthand knowledge of the rhetorical tradition. Waning interest in rhetoric was a widespread social and cultural phenomenon at the end of the nineteenth century. Rhetoric slipped away all but unnoticed from the curricula of the university, and New Testament studies were, in any case, quickly preoccupied with other matters. These preoccupations included the furor over apocalyptic in the teachings of Jesus and the excitement over the new history of religions school with its approach to early Christian myth and ritual. There was also great pressure to shift the scholarly focus from history to hermeneutics. None of the troubled quests for the relevance of the biblical message that dot the history of the twentieth century had much patience for the study of rhetoric. The German movements of theological exegesis (Karl Barth) and existentialist interpretation (Rudolph Bultmann) were even expressly hostile toward rhetorical criticism. In America, interest in Jesus as a teacher of a humane social ethic had little time for cautious reservations about taking his teachings literally. And so the loss of contact with the tradition of rhetorical criticism was not without its reasons. But how, then, was the rediscovery of New Testament rhetoric managed in our time at all?

The new interest in rhetoric is often dated from the presidential address of James Muilenburg to the Society of Biblical Literature in 1968: "After Form Criticism What?" Muilenburg directed his address only to the field of Old Testament studies, his own field of expertise, but his topic was timely for all biblical scholars in the sense that major shifts in scholarly orientation were taking place in general, many of them motivated by a sense that the era of form criticism was over. During the 1970s, for instance, literary criticism caught the imagination of New Testament scholars, parable research became a specialty, pronouncement stories were given concentrated attention, the Passion narratives finally were taken up for rigorous analysis, and the social description of early Christianity suddenly seemed important. The time was surely right for a shifting of the dominant paradigm.

Muilenburg's own answer to the shortfalls of form criticism was a turn to rhetorical criticism. By this he meant the analysis of the formal features of a composition that could take account of authorial accomplishment and creativity. His move was calculated to correct both form-critical assumptions about essentially authorless genres and traditions, as well as fend off the tendency by some literary critics (e.g., the school of New Criticism) to bracket all historical considerations when investigating a text. It was a thoughtful move, and it made a shift in scholarly paradigm (from form to rhetorical-literary criticism) seem right.

Muilenburg's call was not without its precursors. Amos Wilder had already published a startling book, *Early Christian Rhetoric*, written from a literary critic's point of view (1964), and biblical scholars interested in literary criticism were reading such critics as Kenneth Burke (1961, 1969) and Wayne Booth (1961), both of whom had worked to reintroduce rhetoric to literary studies. But neither Muilenburg's call nor Wilder's enticements gave birth to the kind of rhetorical criticism that eventually surfaced in the late 1970s and 1980s in New Testament studies. Muilenburg's notion of rhetoric was limited to matters of style, and his understanding of rhetorical criticism could not encompass a raft of questions already on the horizon about the role of literature within a culture and about the effective difference a piece of writing might make within a given social history. Wilder was more attuned to questions such as these, but his work also primarily affected scholars interested in poetics and the aesthetic effects of style on the imagination, not those interested in a sociology of literature. Muilenburg's call was taken up by Old Testament scholars who merged rhetorical, literary, and structuralist criticisms in a rather esoteric and specialized discourse. Wilder's influence can be followed in the work of those New Testament literary critics who formed the Society of Biblical Literature seminar on parables and generated a discourse within the discipline of biblical studies on the Christian imagination. The new rhetorical criticism did not emerge from either of these scholarly concentrations. It emerged instead from the rough and tumble of the 1970s and the search for a way to move from texts to social histories.

The 1970s marked a very restless scholarship. Literary critics in general were restlessly engaged in efforts to understand their literatures as social, historical, and cultural phenomena. Scholars wanted to know more about the difference a social and cultural history made on the writing of literature, and about the difference a piece of writing might in turn make on society. Old clichés about texts, canons, the history of ideas, aesthetic objects, and the priority of myth over ritual no longer seemed adequate to explain what needed to be explained. Scholars found themselves stunned by the social upheavals of the 1960s and the cultural cross fires of the 1970s. They were embarrassed because they had no theory to account for the effective differences among competing ideologies and political programs. Semantic battles raged over the proper description of world views and social programs, and what to call a given proposal: a myth, an ideal, a system of values, an ideology, a religion, a mystery, or the raving of a demented soul? The proper designation, it seemed, depended upon the social status and perspective of the proponent of a proposal. Thus critical questions had to be phrased in keeping with what Michel Foucault called a society's "discourse," and the boundaries between literary critics and social historians began to erode.

New Testament scholars took to these rapids with amazing alacrity and most managed to ride them out with some sense of exhilaration. No sooner had New Testament critics discovered the New Criticism in the 1960s than structuralism appeared with its promise of a universal theory of narrative and a cultural hermeneutic of discourse. This, however, was quickly followed by a poststructuralist mood of disenchantment when the payoff for particular texts did not always occur. Huge amounts of energy were then expended in exploring the ragged edges of an essentially structuralist vision, looking for ways to control the investigation of the social meaning in texts.

Some of the story has been told in *Semeia*, the experimental journal of the Society of Biblical Literature. There have been special issues devoted to structuralism, semiotics, linguistics, narrative theory, theory of oral transmission, cultural anthropology, theory of religion, social-scientific criticism, theory of writing, reader-response criticism, social context hermeneutics, and more—all oriented to New Testament texts and the question of how to understand them in their several social and cultural contexts. The desire to understand a text had moved beyond the delineation of aesthetic, meditative, and theological reflections. The streamers from this explosion of intellectual energy spread out in all directions, seeking conversation with both the humanities and the social sciences. The many investigations have had a singular purpose, namely, to position a literary performance at some juncture of social history and assess its effectiveness as a moment of communication and significant human exchange. That quest was the intellectual circumstance that called for the modern rhetorical criticism of the New Testament.

In 1969, John Wilkinson and Purcell Weaver of the Center for the Study of Democratic Institutions published an English translation of Chaim Perelman and L. Olbrechts-Tyteca's French-language treatise, *The New Rhetoric: A Treatise on Argumentation*. This book quickly caught the attention of scholars interested in rhetoric and soon became the handbook of reference for all who wanted to apply the rules of rhetoric to the criticism of literature.

Perelman and Olbrechts-Tyteca were relentless in their definition and discussion of rhetorical strategies as argumentation. This fact alone is sufficient to mark their study as a historic moment of intellectual history. Defining rhetoric as argumentation countered a cultural sensibility, keenly cultivated for almost two thousand years, that regarded rhetoric mainly as a matter of stylistic ornamentation. Rhetoric acquired this particular

14

nuance during the second sophistic when the civic institutions of the Roman world had ceased to provide a forum for active and meaningful public debate. Rhetoric as style was cultivated consciously for the long reaches of Christian history, both in its Eastern and Western forms. It was still the dominant notion when Bultmann, troubled about Paul's *kunstmässige* (artfully crafted) rhetoric in defense of the gospel, wrote his dissertation, *Der Stil der paulinischen Predigt und die stoisch-kynische Diatribe*, in 1910. By emphasizing argumentation, Perelman and Olbrechts-Tyteca revived the ancient classical definition of rhetoric as "the art of persuasion," described a logic of communication that could be applied to widely ranging modes of human discourse, and immersed the study of speech events in social situations.

The second observation to be made about Perelman and Olbrechts-Tyteca's book is that they succeeded in demonstrating the importance of the situation or speech context when calculating the persuasive force of an argumentation. Many scholars have noted that this feature of their treatise is a truly new contribution to theory of argumentation. If one were to think of the rhetorical equation in terms of the relations among speaker, speech, and audience, the special contribution by Perelman and Olbrechts-Tyteca would be an elaboration of the factors that impinge upon the speaker-audience relationship. They worked these out in terms of fine distinctions used to describe a social-historical circumstance. Literary critics saw the chance to revive old interests in the works of Kenneth Burke and to begin to bridge the gap between literary criticism and social history. New Testament scholars also quickly made the connection to a number of concerns within their own field of study. One concern was to better understand the contribution of a text's "setting in life" for the meaning of a text. Another was the growing interest in "sociological exegesis," or the way in which one might study a literary text in the interest of reconstructing its social history of context. Perelman and Olbrechts-Tyteca had offered a no-nonsense way of talking about the persuasive power of various modes of discourse in the real world. Literary critics, including New Testament critics, followed their lead and learned to read their own texts in terms of the rhetorical equation.

This leads to a third observation about the importance of this book. By linking the persuasive power of a speech not only to its logic of argumentation, but to the manner in which it addresses the social and cultural history of its audience and speaker, Perelman and Olbrechts-Tyteca demonstrated the rhetorical coefficient that belongs to every human exchange involving speech, including common conversation and the daily discourse of a working society. This takes rhetoric out of the sphere of mere ornamentation, embellished literary style, and the extravagances

15

of public oratory, and places it at the center of a social theory of language. On this model, rhetorical performance belongs to human discourse just as surely as stance and style belong to any presentation of ourselves at moments of personal encounter. Rhetoric is to a society and its discourse what grammar is to a culture and its language. Rhetoric refers to the rules of the language games agreed upon as acceptable within a given society. The rules of a rhetoric can be identified and studied, just as the rules of a grammar. Interest in such a rhetoric is grounded in the observation that the way we talk to each other is very serious business. Rhetorical theory defines the stakes as nothing less than the negotiation of our lives together. A criticism based upon such a theory of rhetoric might hope to get to the heart of the human matter.

Thus the title of Perelman and Olbrechts-Tyteca's book is accurate. It is indeed a "new rhetoric"—new because of the theoretical advances they made; new because they challenged the reigning definition of rhetoric as mainly a matter of style; new because for many of their readers rhetoric had hardly been a consideration at all. And yet, as any scholar with some acquaintance with the classical traditions knows, the new rhetoric is actually a rediscovery of the old. The old rhetoric was also a "treatise on argumentation" based on the discriminating observance of discourse in the social sphere. The Greeks took a fancy to the game of public debate, noticed the skill required to participate in public forum, worked out the rules, and called it the art of speaking (*technē rhetorikē*). They thought that knowing the rules would enhance the practice and hone the performance of speaking persuasively and well. They produced handbooks for teaching this technology, an archive of practical knowledge, educational syllabi, and models for mimesis (imitation). They also cultivated occasions for playing the game of repartee, developed a satire capable of bringing critique to rhetorical performance, and created a culture thoroughly at ease with its knowledge that all discourse was rhetorical.

The importance of this fact for New Testament studies cannot be overemphasized. If the new rhetoric is actually a rearticulation of the old rhetoric, a modern criticism commends itself that is curiously appropriate to the culture of context within which the literature under investigation was written. In the course of the scholarly investigation of the New Testament, a pursuit that is highly conscious of itself as a historiography, there have been many attempts to describe its cultures of context. The usual approach has been to set the texts of the New Testament alongside the literatures others produced, both Jews and Greeks, during the Greco-Roman period, in order to elucidate the distinctive ideas of the early Christian movements. But other indexes of the cultures of context have regularly been studied or assumed as well. These include philosophies, theologies, religious systems, and political histories. Now the study of rhetoric can be added to this list of significant ways to describe the Hellenistic age. Insofar as the development of a theory of rhetoric indicates a society conscious of its culture, an amazing opportunity does present itself to catch Jews, Greeks, and early Christians thinking out loud. The name for this new historiography, an approach to texts with an eye to social histories, is not yet firmly established among scholars. But some are content to call it "rhetorical criticism."

There is no guarantee that rhetorical criticism will fulfill its promise of helping to bridge the gap between a literature and its social history. Progress will depend upon the way in which scholarship takes its lead. Until recently the impasse between literary critics uninterested in social history and social historians uninterested in the poetics of imagination was stark. This regrettable division of labor in the study of early Christian literature and history is no longer acceptable and some scholars trained in each approach have been seeking ways to contribute to a common endeavor. Rhetorical criticism should therefore prove helpful, for it allows a text to be read both ways. It can plunge a writing back into its social setting, not only to be used as a window for viewing other social facets, but as a social factor of significance itself. Rhetorical criticism can turn a literary production into the protocol of a persuasion without rejecting other ways of viewing its accomplishments. Rhetorical criticism can place a writing at a juncture of social history and read it as a record of some moment of exchange that may have contributed to the social formations we seek better to understand. Rhetorical criticism may be in fact the most promising form of literary criticism for the task of reconstructing Christian origins with social issues in view. It will no doubt be asked to try.

This book is offered as an introduction and guide to the recent scholarship in rhetorical criticism. It is already clear that it must include the following items: a brief survey of the most recent New Testament scholarship on rhetorical criticism (Part I); an overview of the classical theory and practice of rhetoric (Part II); a sizable number of illustrations, taken from the New Testament, in which rhetorical composition and argumentation can be demonstrated (Part III); reflection on the promise of rhetorical criticism (Conclusion); and, finally, a bibliography for those who wish to join in the pursuit.

I
The Rise of
a Critical Discipline

Since the mid-1970s, rhetorical studies of early Jewish and Christian texts have burgeoned. A certain élan is to be noticed, though there is no single network of scholars in conversation about the approach—no school, acknowledged master, or canon of methods at the center of this activity. It is also the case that there has been no programmatic essay or slogan to announce its presence. And only infrequently has it even occurred to anyone to attempt an explanation for the rest of the guild of biblical scholars as to why rhetorical criticism may be important. That being the case, a description of this scholarship is best sketched in broad profile by organizing the rather unruly bibliography around a number of recurring themes or emphases. This approach will, unfortunately, not allow for a celebration of any given individual's contribution. But it does allow us to offer an overview of an emerging enterprise that is developing distinctive characteristics and a reasonably tough texture. It also aids us in identifying those characteristics of this scholarly enterprise that mark it as a potentially significant discipline.

A. THE TURN TOWARD ARGUMENTATION

The single most important feature of the new rhetorical criticism is a clarity about rhetoric as argumentation. As mentioned above, rhetoric had long been regarded mainly as a matter of style, ornamentation, and manipulation, not as the rules by which debate, argumentation, and discourse proceed. The older understanding was easily integrated into the study of literature as part and parcel of an *ars poetica,* and it was an *ars poetica,* not an *ars rhetorica,* that still held sway over the critical imagination during the early 1970s. In this tradition, the study of rhetorical tropes (figures of speech) was understood merely to enhance other hermeneutical interests by identifying locations where language worked its magic and the mystery of meaning might show through. Students of rhetoric must still pay close attention to the figural features of a text, of course, and rhetorical critics are still to be found lingering over a turn of phrase just as literary critics have always done. But rhetorical analysis is no longer limited to the observance of aesthetic literary objects and their effect upon the imagination. Rhetorical criticism is now distinguished by its attention to the art of persuasion and its effect upon the judgments one must make in the course of living together as social creatures.

One sign of the shift in interest from rhetoric as ornamentation to rhetoric as argumentation is the frequency with which the book by Chaim Perelman and L. Olbrechts-Tyteca, *The New Rhetoric*, is cited in recent biblical scholarship. The subtitle of this book is *A Treatise on Argumentation*. Another is a noticeable increase in reference to the classical tradition of rhetoric where argumentation was the major concern. In this case, the handbook by Heinrich Lausberg (1960) has proven to be an indispensable guide to the primary texts. Biblical scholars use its system of classification regularly as a short-hand code to technical terminology and explanatory discussions of the classical handbooks. And a third sign of the shift is the way in which biblical scholars have begun to set forth their research in the rhetoricity of New Testament texts. Not only is it commonly assumed that rhetoric is to be defined as the art of persuasion, scholars tend to treat their texts as moments of social-historical consequence. In this scholarship, it is understood, the rhetorical situation has to be reconstructed, the issue that mattered has to be identified, and the designs of the authors upon their listeners/readers have to be disclosed.

Important contributions to rhetorical criticism as an analysis of argumentation have been made by Wilhelm Wuellner (1976, 1979, 1987), R. Wonneberger (1976), Karl Blumauer (1979), Hans-Dieter Betz (1979, 1986), Burton L. Mack (1984, 1987), Folker Siegert (1985), G. Smiga (1985), and Bruce Johanson (1987). Wuellner's 1987 essay, "Where is Rhetorical Criticism Taking Us?" offers the best and most pointed discussion of the shift and its significance. Wuellner is, in fact, a strong advocate for working out the definition of the discipline in terms of rhetoric as argumentation. His article offers a fine point of entry into this recent scholarly discourse. Here the reader will not only find an introduction to other recent literature related to rhetorical criticism but will also catch the flavor of a technical terminology in the process of development.

The other studies mentioned above do not address the larger context of modern scholarship in the same way as Wuellner. They do, however, contain detailed explications of rhetoric and its logic of argumentation.

Each author finds it necessary to do this as preparation for some particular exegetical endeavor, as, for instance, Betz on Galatians, Mack on the pronouncement stories, and Siegert on Romans. Each study can therefore be taken as a self-conscious example of the new criticism and its orientation to rhetoric as the art of persuasion.

Additionally, an emerging body of studies has focused upon particular techniques used by Paul: analyses of antithesis (Schneider, 1970), use of scriptural citations (Wuellner, 1978), lexical choice (Silva, 1980), rhetorical employment of epistolary formula (Buenker, 1984), use of hyperbole (DuToit, 1985), use of rhetorical questions (Wuellner, 1986), rhetorical use of the theme of boasting (Forbes, 1986), and rhetorical use of the theme of mimesis (Castelli, 1987). In these studies technique is understood as craft in the service of persuasion, not merely as creativity in the interest of cleverness, aesthetics, or the enhancement of mysterious meanings. The turn toward rhetoric as argumentation is the single most important feature of this new rhetorical criticism.

B. THE DISCOVERY OF RHETORICAL UNITS

A second distinguishing feature of the new rhetorical criticism is an orientation to blocks or units of material rather than to occasional instances of figures, tropes, ideas, or themes. Argumentation usually implies the making of several points, normally in a set pattern or sequence, and frequently in a tightly knit unit of composition. It is therefore not surprising that scholars of the newer rhetorical criticism have automatically selected for their work literary units that exhibit recognizable patterns of argumentation.

This feature marks the point at which rhetorical analysis may complement or compete with the more traditional interests of literary criticism in questions of form and genre. One of the lasting contributions of form criticism, for instance, was to draw scholarly attention to the importance of smaller literary units for larger literary compositions in late antiquity. Delimiting the pericope or textual unit for investigation is now expected of the critical scholar, and this standard operation has been guided primarily by form- and literary-critical criteria. Rhetorical observations add other criteria for determining the form, structure, and scope of a literary unit of composition. In some cases, the identification of a rhetorical unit has had a striking effect upon its description as a literary unit. In other cases, the definition of a unit on literary-critical grounds has been accepted, then submitted to rhetorical analysis.

Important in this regard is the large number of studies that have identified textual units of argumentation in the letters of Paul. All of these studies have followed a line of argumentation throughout a textual unit, and each has made the attempt to account for all of the material in the unit in relation to the line of argument. The units vary in size from a chapter or two to entire letters. The list includes studies in the Thessalonian correspondence (Hughes, 1984; Jewett, 1987, Johanson, 1987), Galatians (Betz, 1979; Brinsmead, 1982; Huebner, 1984; Hester, 1984, 1986; Smiga, 1985; Kraftchick, 1985), the Corinthian correspondence (Standaert, 1983; Betz, 1985), Romans (Scroggs, 1976; Wuellner, 1976; Stowers, 1981; Jewett, 1982; Siegert, 1985), Philippians (Watson, 1984), and Philemon (Church, 1978; Petersen, 1985).

Several scholars have also discovered units of argumentation in the Jesus traditions, most notably, units that follow the pattern some rhetors called an elaboration. Earlier work on the pronouncement stories as units of elaboration by Vernon K. Robbins (1982, 1983, 1985, 1987), Charles Reedy (1983), James Butts (1983), Burton L. Mack (1984, 1987), and Rod Parrott (1985) is now coming to fruition in detailed and constructive analyses of material in Q. One fine example is the study by Ron Cameron (1988) on John and Jesus in Luke 7:18-35. A formal discussion of this pattern and its application to synoptic materials can be found in Mack (1984, 1987) and Mack and Robbins (1989). The importance here, in distinction from the work on rhetorical units in the letters, is that aphoristic, proverbial, and figural material, traditionally viewed as "free floating logia" and normally understood not to have logical or argumentative significance, can be shown to cluster in cleverly designed units of argumentation.

As for the Gospels as whole literary units, Robbins (1984) and Mack (1988) have investigated Mark from a rhetorical point of view. George Kennedy has offered a few observations on the rhetoric of the Gospels in *New Testament Interpretation through Rhetorical Criticism* (1985, chap. 5), and Jeffrey Staley has launched a rhetorical investigation of the implied reader in the Fourth Gospel (1988). Important work also has been done on the sermons in Acts as rhetorical units of argumentation by Wills (1984) and Black (1988). And the rhetoric of Hebrews has recently been emphasized by Harold Attridge (1989). The impression overall, therefore, is that the range of New Testament texts amenable to rhetorical criticism can no longer be limited to the letters of Paul. Pauline studies continue to dominate the scene, as one might expect. But significant forays are now under way into all forms of New Testament literature, including Q, the Gospels, Acts, Hebrews, and the non-Pauline epistles, as well as many other noncanonical early Christian and Jewish writings. These studies are surely to be taken as announcements that the rhetorical analysis of early Christian and Jewish literature is about to begin in earnest.

C. ENCOUNTERING THE QUESTION OF AUTHORITY

Rhetorical criticism cannot avoid the question of the stature of the speaker and his or her right to speak and be heard. In the study of early Christian literature this question is compounded by rhetoric with high polemical coefficient and outright debates over authority. Studies that have probed these issues by means of rhetorical analyses are particularly helpful, if poignant, including the studies of Galatians by Kraftchick (1985) and Hester (1984, 1986), and the analysis of the pronouncement stories by Mack (1988, chap. 7). Devastating critiques of the rhetoric by which Paul laid claim to authority have been given by Graham Shaw (1983) and Elizabeth Castelli (1987). As one might expect, studies such as these have raised the issue not only of the locus of authority for the truth of the gospel but also of the relationship between the truth of the gospel and the rhetoric used to defend it.

These issues have evoked a number of studies that compare the logic implicit in rhetorical argumentation with the theological assumptions implicit in early Christian propositions. Some scholars have tackled this problem more in terms of the age-old debate between faith and reason, notably A. T. Hanson (1974), Dieter Kemmler (1975), and Karl Blumauer (1979). Others have made the attempt to define two types of logic, one according to which rhetorical argument moves, the other peculiar to the privileged claims of the Christian gospel. Examples of the latter would be Betz's introduction to the Galatians commentary (1979) and his recent article, "The Problem of Rhetoric and Theology according to the Apostle Paul" (1986), three excursuses in Siegert's study of Romans (1985), and some remarks that Kennedy made in his general introduction to the rhetoric of the New Testament (1984).

Kennedy's solution to the curious mix of myth and logic in early Christian discourse was to bracket the fundamental assertions of Christians as the "radical rhetoric" of religious or "sacred" language and limit discussion to the way in which other, more normal considerations were introduced as arguments in support of these claims. This approach is obviously not satisfying, but the issue is sensitive and will therefore require a great amount of patient probing. The center of concern, it seems, will have to shift away from orientation to philosophical or religious claims to truth and toward the arena of social formation where the effective difference of a given claim can be described and evaluated. In the meantime, the student of rhetorical criticism can certainly come to a better understanding of the situation by noting the variety of early Christian persuasions and by tracing each persuasion to its own configuration of authorities. Eventually, rhetorical criticism may be called upon to rank the various

23

authorities to which early Christians appealed and evaluate them in terms of their persuasive force from various social perspectives.

D. ENGAGING SOCIAL HISTORIES

The move from rhetorical analysis to the social setting of a text is not yet a dominant feature of this scholarship. It is no doubt too soon to expect elaborate reconstructions of the social implications uncovered in the investigation of a rhetorical situation. There have been already a number of promising explorations, however, and these deserve emphasis. They include Stowers's fine article, "Social Status, Public Speaking and Private Teaching: The Circumstance of Paul's Preaching Activity" (1984), Betz's study of the social circumstance for 2 Corinthians 8 and 9 (1985), a remarkable twenty pages on rhetorical criticism tucked away in the middle of Norman Petersen's very exciting study of the sociology of Philemon (1985), Wuellner's article, "Paul as Pastor" (1986), Mack's work on the pronouncement stories in Mark (1988, chap. 7), and Mack on the social history of the Q people (1988).

These four features of the new rhetorical criticism indicate the direction this guidebook must take. There should be some introduction to classical rhetoric, including theory of argumentation, as well as some account of the social role and cultural significance of rhetoric during the classical and Hellenistic periods. Such an introduction is given in part II.

The major portion of the book should be devoted to illustrations of rhetorical argumentation in the New Testament. These need to be taken from a wide range of literary traditions and genres. They should implicate authorial design, demonstrate patterns of argumentation, and address issues that have social consequence. Sixteen examples of New Testament rhetorical composition are given in part III.

In the conclusion, a brief description of early Christian discourse can be given, based upon the rhetoric discovered in the examples presented. This will lead to a meditation on the promise of rhetorical analysis as a critical discipline and its challenge to traditional biblical hermeneutics.

II

The Classical Tradition
as Cultural Context

Recognizing the use of rhetoric in the New Testament requires some acquaintance with the practice of rhetoric during the Greco-Roman period. Three areas are critical for this task. First, one needs some sense of the place of rhetoric, its importance, and its pervasive influence in first-century society and culture. This is important in order to understand how early Christian authors came into contact with rhetorical practice. Second, one needs some knowledge of the forms of rhetorical speech and their several patterns of argumentation. This is important in order to discern units of rhetorical composition in the New Testament. Third, it is necessary to grasp the principles of rhetorical proof (in distinction from philosophical demonstration). This is important in order to evaluate the New Testament use of maxims, metaphors, examples, and scriptural citations as proofs that count in a pattern of argumentation. This chapter provides an orientation to each of these requirements.

A. A BRIEF HISTORY OF CLASSICAL RHETORIC

1. The Greek Origins

Rhetoric emerged in the rough-and-tumble of the Greek city-states during the sixth and fifth centuries B.C.E. Legend has it that rhetoric was the force that banished the tyrants and gave the Greeks democracy (see Farenga, 1979). History has it that debate was natural and necessary in the councils of the oligarchies and the assemblies of the people *(demos)*, and that the rules of rhetoric were learned by trial, error, and inventiveness (see Clark, 1957; Kennedy, 1963). Since there were no lawyers, individual citizens had to come to speech for themselves on all matters of public policy, law, and litigation. Some Greeks took note, conceptualized the process, and started to analyze the ways with words that worked.

The earliest names associated with the history of rhetoric are Corax and Tisias, residents of the Greek colony of Syracuse. Stories of democratic struggles against tyrannies in the Greek colonies of Sicily and of a major dispute about the use of public property in Syracuse paint the background for the leading roles of these rhetors and their development of rhetorical techniques. Gorgias, also from Sicily, is sometimes given credit for introducing rhetoric to Athens on the occasion of an embassy in 427 from his hometown, Leontini, a Greek colony not far from Syracuse. In this case, the magic of his antitheses and oratorical style caught the imagination of the Athenians and created the excitement for a vigorous investigation of the role of speech making in the polis. By the end of the century the foundations had been laid for three different traditions of rhetorical theory and practice: sophistic, philosophical, and technical.

The sophists were entrepreneurs of private education in the personal skills required for success in the competitive arena of the Greek city-state. Following Gorgias, who himself had accepted students, sophists added rhetoric to their curricula. They offered instruction in the practical approach to persuasive speech, providing students with model speeches, mnemonic techniques, and strategies for winning arguments in public forum. Their pragmatic approach to individual freedom and their promises of success resulted in a reputation for unprincipled pursuit of selfish aims, at least in the eyes of some schools of philosophy. Among the sophists, however, were gifted intellectuals like Hippias of Elis, Protagoras, and Isocrates, who were fully and constructively engaged in the life of the polis and deeply concerned about issues of public policy. Sophists also played an important role in the expansion of the Greek system of education during the Hellenistic period, serving as personal tutors, setting up private schools, and teaching in public schools throughout the eastern Mediterranean. Nevertheless, the image of the itinerant sophist and his public displays of rhetorical cleverness continued into the Roman period and regularly were reprimanded by philosophically minded writers such as Philo of Alexandria.

Isocrates, a student of Gorgias, also looked askance at the cheaper brands of sophistry and integrated the study of technique with the practice of rhetoric by founding a professional school. His school, begun in the 390s, greatly influenced the subsequent history of education, not only by providing the model for higher education in rhetoric and civics but also by setting the curriculum for secondary schools focused primarily upon a rhetorical approach to literature.

In the philosophic tradition of the Academy and Lyceum, sophists were viewed with suspicion. Their liberal, pragmatic, and entrepreneurial approach to education was not grounded in a prior commitment to a philosophical concept of justice (Socrates), truth (Plato), or logic (Aristotle). This issue, the conflict between rhetoric and philosophy, was to exercise the best minds of Greek and Roman antiquity. It raised the question of ethics caught between individual and collective interests, or where to locate authority and power in the construction of a democratic society. Philosophers preferred arrangements for law and order based on rational and idealistic models of the city-state, and they pointed out that rhetoric could easily be misused by unprincipled persons and thus was not suitable for building a solid foundation for a just and sustainable society. The sophists however, did contribute to the construction of a democratic society. And they also had profound affect upon subsequent philosophical agenda. They had introduced the question of language and discourse into the humanities. After the discovery of rhetoric, no philosophical tradition could discuss the process of knowing and thinking without taking a position with regard to the function and limits of language. The Socratic method of dialogue, bringing a person to puzzlement *(aporia)* in the quest for truth; Plato's method of dialectic *(diairesis)*, the process of intellectual ascent to abstract ideas; and Aristotle's program of analytics, whereby the logics of thinking and making judgments was worked out, were all indebted to the conceptualization of discourse *(dialexis)* as rhetorical argumentation *(dialektikē)*.

Actual evidence for the third tradition of rhetoric, the tradition that produced the technical handbooks, is less abundant for this early period. The social settings for the transmission of technical handbooks are even less clear. Plato, however, mentions such books in Athens of the fifth century, and Aristotle's treatise, "The Art of Rhetoric," a study in the relation of the logic of persuasion (rhetoric) to the logic of demonstration (philosophical dialectic), makes use of earlier texts. Aristotle's treatise has become the classic statement on ancient rhetoric for modern scholars, but it was hardly the norm for the technical tradition in antiquity. His treatise was as a matter of fact lost from view, tucked away perhaps in the library of the Lyceum, until Cicero claimed to merge Aristotle's theory of rhetoric with the technical tradition in the first century B.C.E. Only one other technical handbook is extant from the late classical and Hellenistic periods, the *Rhetorica ad Alexandrum* (early third century), but others are known (or thought) to have been written by rhetors such as Isocrates (fourth century) and Hermagoras of Temnos (mid-second century). Special studies on aspects of rhetoric (e.g., style) were also produced, both at the Lyceum and at large. Evidence for the strength and richness of this tradition exists in a a first-century (B.C.E.) work, *Rhetorica ad Herennium,* a Latin handbook that reproduces an eclectic composite of various Greek traditions, some of which hark back to the pre-Aristotelian classical period. Thus there can be no doubt that technical rhetoric was pursued vigorously from the first, and that handbooks were in use wherever advanced instruction was offered throughout the Greco-Roman world.

By the first century B.C.E., the practice of rhetoric had been thoroughly enculturated, the system of techniques fully explored, the logic rationalized, and the pedagogy refined. Rhetoric permeated both the system of education and the manner of public discourse that marked the culture of Hellenism on the eve of the Roman age.

2. Rhetoric in the First Century C.E.

Rhetoric emerged in the city-state under the banner of "freedom, citizenship, and autonomy." The forum for the practice of rhetoric was the assembly *(ekklēsia)* or the council *(boulē)* gathered for deliberation and litigation, or the public gathering for celebration of civic-religious occasions. Thus the rhetors distinguished three major types of speech: the deliberative, the judicial, and the ceremonial (or epideictic). With Philip of Macedonia's victory over Athens and Thebes at the battle of Chaeronea in 338 B.C.E., however, the political picture was rearranged, the power of the prince was reintroduced, and the Hellenistic period began. Founding cities on the Greek model was the major means of disseminating Greek culture under Alexander and his successors, but the Hellenistic city was now used to insure imperial control, and each city was linked by charter and largesse to one of the centers of power where kings resided with their armies. For Palestine this meant either Alexandria (during the third century) or Antioch (during the second and first centuries). Citizenship had to be redefined and granted, for complicated mixtures of ethnic decent and indigenous population were now the rule. Judicial rhetoric could still be practiced in local Hellenistic courts, but these courts were not "supreme," and the questions of jurisdiction and appeal to higher authority changed the tenor of the trial process. Occasions and topics for deliberation and for oratorical display also differed from those of the classical period in Greece. Thus shifts occurred in both the practice and theory of rhetoric that tamed it for imperial civilization.

One such shift was an increased interest in style and oratorical finesse. A second was the domestication of deliberative rhetoric for use in the classroom where all manner of subjects could be debated theoretically. A third was the development of a speech form called the declamation, used in lectures for instruction and in public for display. When the Romans took charge in the first century B.C.E., yet another imperial structure and judicial system (with professional advocates) that further modified the practice of rhetoric was superimposed upon the civic process. Eventually, rhetoric was shorn of the critical thrust and political nuance characteristic of its origins. Rhetoric was now in the service of culture. It could be used to defend, manifest, and inculcate virtues and values held to be noble, an ethos that celebrated its derivation by idealizing the classical period and imitating its style. Scholars call this development the "second sophistic."

What these shifts meant for the cultural situation in Palestine during the first century C.E. deserves a brief description. Greek cities dotted the landscape around the eastern Mediterranean. We know of at least 350 cities founded during the Hellenistic and early Roman period. In Palestine alone there were over thirty Hellenistic cities during the time of Jesus, twelve within a twenty-five-mile radius of Nazareth. Greek cities had gymnasia (schools) and theaters. The remains of twenty Greek theaters have been unearthed by archaeologists in Palestine, one at Sepphoris, three miles north of Nazareth. The gymnasium, theater, and market (agora) were all traditional and popular places for speech making. Visiting dignitaries, civic leaders, teachers, and performers would be asked to address the people. Hellenistic culture was a culture of rhetoric and rhetoric was clearly a public affair (see Kinneavy, 1987, chap. 3).

Thus the vehicles of high culture were dispersed throughout the Greco-Roman world. An important question, therefore, is whether these vehicles are to be understood as road shows or as centers that contributed to the cultivation and reproduction of Greek culture, albeit on foreign soil. The usual picture is that Athens was still important as a center for higher education, but that other leading cities soon took their places as centers for Greek learning as well, including Rhodes, Pergamum, Antioch, and Alexandria. This picture is not incorrect, but it is inadequate to account for the phenomenon of leading figures in all of the arts and sciences who were born, raised, and took up residence for their work in smaller Hellenistic cities throughout this world. Gadara, a city of the Decapolis about twenty miles east of Nazareth, is an example of this phenomenon. Already in the third century B.C.E., Gadara could boast of the Cynic poet Menippus. From the first century B.C.E., Philodemus, an Epicurean rhetorician, the Cynic epigrammatist Meleager, and Theodorus, rhetorician and eventually tutor to Tiberius, were all from Gadara. The same story could be told of many other Hellenistic cities in the Levant, leading to the conclusions that Greek culture had firmly taken root throughout the eastern Mediterranean, and that the institutions of its dissemination were effective. These institutions were decidedly open-air arrangements, producing activities for all to see and hear. Greek culture *(paideia)* and public education *(paideia)* were one and the same.

The Hellenistic school was divided into three levels. Elementary education was offered to *paides* (children, both boys and girls to fourteen years of age). The curriculum consisted of reading, writing, literature, arithmetic, music, and physical exercises. Secondary education was offered to *epheboi* (both young men and women, ages fifteen to seventeen). It focused on literature, math, and science, with literature emphasized as the means for cultural inculcation. During the first century B.C.E. through the first century C.E., rhetoric began to be introduced at this level of education. Special handbooks for teachers of the "first exercises" in rhetoric (later called *progymnasmata*) were written in such a way that a student could move by degrees from the rhetorical analysis of literature that was already familiar to the principles and practice of specifically rhetorical compositions such as speeches.

Higher education began at age eighteen. At this point, young men and women who were able went off to professional schools. Schools of philosophy were still the standard for the advanced pursuit of the humanities. But the schools of rhetoric provided the training for a greater range of professions. Teachers, lawyers, public officials, civic leaders of all kinds, and those who aspired to some form of literary profession, either as a writer or as a "grammarian" (or research scholar) under patronage of some private or civic library, were well served by rhetorical education. Other professions, such as the practice of medicine, were learned by apprenticeship.

One of the results of the merger of rhetoric and literature was that the classics (Homer, Hesiod, Theognis, the poets, historians, and tragedians) were studied for their use of rhetorical techniques. Another result was that the composition of literature other than speeches began to reflect studied attention to rhetorical principles. Plutarch's *Lives* and *Moralia* offer good examples of this, as do the commentaries of Philo of Alexandria, the discourses of Dio Chrysostom, and the letters of Seneca. If we place the writings of the New Testament in this larger cultural context, we should not be surprised to discover patterns of rhetorical composition within them as well.

Rhetoric defined the technology of discourse customary for all who participated in the culture of the Greco-Roman age. This technology could be learned. Whether one became highly skilled as a rhetor, or merely a competent critic of one's times, one knew that the rules of discourse were firm, achievements were recognizable, and cheating at the game of persuasion was dangerous. Formal education may have been costly and thus not available to many. But the products of the Hellenistic school were not private commodities. They were fully public affairs. Techniques of rhetoric were tested in the public arena, just as were performances in music, literature, gymnastics, theater, and so on. The agora, the gymnasium, and the theatre, as well as the family courtyard and the city chambers, were all good places to give and hear an interesting speech. Speech and speeches were signs of the presence of Hellenistic culture. All people, whether formally trained or not, were fully schooled in the wily ways of sophists, the eloquence required at civic festivals, the measured tones of the local teacher, and the heated debates where differences of opinion battled for the right to say what should be done. To be engulfed in the culture of Hellenism meant to have ears trained for the rhetoric of speech. Rhetoric provided the rules for making critical judgments in the course of all forms of social intercourse. Early Christians were not unskilled, either as critics of their cultures of context or as proponents of their own emerging persuasions.

B. CLASSICAL THEORY AND TECHNIQUE

There are three bodies of literature that serve as a resource for the study of the classical theory of rhetoric: (1) the primary texts consisting mainly of technical handbooks (for professionals), *progymnasmata* (for intermediate school teachers), and later commentaries upon them (mainly in the Byzantine tradition of scholasticism); (2) studies by modern scholars on the classical tradition; and (3) modern handbooks that condense the corpus of classical handbooks for the ready reference of technical terms. Our bibliography lists the major texts in each of these classifications. Most of the classical handbooks are conveniently available in the Loeb Classical Library. Special attention should be given to Aristotle's *Ars Rhetorica*, Cicero's *De inventione*, and the *Rhetorica ad Herennium*. Important also are the *progymnasmata* of Theon and Hermogenes. These, unfortunately, are not as readily available, either in Greek or in English translation. Reference in this guide, therefore, will be made only to the chapters on the chreia in Theon and Hermogenes, available in the publication by Ron Hock and Edward O'Neil. For those who wish to pursue the study of rhetoric seriously, the recommended modern text is *The New Rhetoric* by Chaim Perelman and L. Olbrechts-Tyteca. This descriptive treatise has become a standard reference work for scholars working with the rhetorical theory of argumentation.

1. The Classical Handbooks

The purpose of the handbook was to organize knowledge about the art of persuasion for teachers of higher education and advanced practitioners. In general, five aspects of the practice of rhetoric were addressed. These were called invention, arrangement, style, memory, and delivery.

(a) Invention *(heuresis, inventio)* referred to the conceptual process of deciding on the subject to be elaborated, the position one would take on an issue of debate, or the thesis one wished to propose. It also referred to the search for materials one might use in developing the speech and to the selection of techniques best suited to support one's position. Since the process of invention was understood to be more a matter of finding or discovering the right material for making a point, and less a matter of creating a brand-new idea, the classical handbooks contained lists of stock figures to guide the search. The principles of organization for these lists were diverse and depended to some extent upon the kind of material to be exemplified. Standard techniques, basic types of argument, conventional figures of speech, forms of fallacious argumentation, famous literary citations, and stock images were types of material that the rhetors organized for discussion by creating various kinds of lists. The items in these lists were called *topoi* ("places"). The term *topoi* could be used as well to refer to the list itself as a classification of material with generic significance. "Invention" was thus imagined as a search for the right "place" (or pigeonhole) from which to take a "topic" for a particular rhetorical purpose.

One form of invention in early Christian circles would be the practice of searching the Scriptures to find just the right example, maxim, proverb, oracle, or legal precedent for a given argument. This would have been a challenging test of ingenuity, for the Jewish Scriptures had to be reinterpreted even while being claimed as proofs for Christian propositions. A fine example is the use of the story about what David did in the controversy over plucking grain on the Sabbath (see Part III, Section 2). One can see that this story was chosen with extreme care and caution. It was invented in order to claim epic precedence for early Christian practice even while highlighting a case of incongruence within Jewish tradition, an incongruence held to be embarrassing for one's Jewish opponents.

(b) Arrangement *(taxis, dispositio)* referred to the work of ordering this material into an outline, paying attention to such things as the best sequence to use, or whether one should expand upon this or that point, or how best to develop a subtheme. Skeletal outlines for the several types of speech were standard, and these will be discussed below. Skeletal outlines helped to get the arrangement of material started for a given composition. But rhetors were expected to hide the standard outline when crafting a speech, and to produce a composition that would appear to unfold naturally on a given occasion. Arrangement was as important and creative a process as invention. In actual practice, each influenced the other in the work of composition.

All of the examples to follow in chapter 3 demonstrate the facility of early Christian authors in the arrangement of rhetorical compositions. The point can be made quite simply by reference to the many instances in the synoptic traditions where the same smaller units of material occur in different arrangements in different literary contexts. A good example is the rearrangement of Q material in Matthew's Sermon on the Mount, an arrangement that bristles with obvious rhetorical strategy (see Part III, Section 13).

(c) Style (lexis, elocutio) referred to the way in which one handled the material in the process of composition. Basic considerations of grammar, syntax, and the selection of words with just the right denotation or connotation were treated as important matters. Clarity was frequently mentioned as all-important. Figures of speech were discussed in relation to their appropriateness for the various kinds of speeches. Metaphors, for instance, were considered distracting at critical junctures in a judicial argument, but appropriate and helpful in encomiastic oratory. The choice of "plain," "middle," or "heightened" (eloquent, poetic prose) style was an important consideration. Under the rubric of style one also learned about the relative virtues of "periodic" and "continuous" discourse, or the way in which transitions between sentences and blocks of material might be crafted. Style was understood to be both a matter of aesthetic effect and an important factor in persuasion. Style was considered a clue to the "ethos" (character or trustworthiness) of the speaker as well as a primary means for creating "pathos," or the desired effect upon the audience. Style had to fit the purpose and occasion of the speech.

Early Christians were alert to the problem of style. Mark's reference to Jesus' authority and Paul's disavowal of eloquence were stylistic observations pertinent to the issue of how an audience might respond to their messages. In general, early Christian rhetoric was marked by unusual claims to authority, claims intended to enhance the privileged status and seriousness of the message even while creating imposing obstacles to its entertainment. Early Christians capitalized in this way on the novelty of their message and developed a number of styles that matched its sharp leading edge. For instance, Jesus' teaching in the earlier layers of Q is highly imperatival, a style fitting the status of Jesus' authority for these tradents at this juncture of their history (see Part III, Sections 1, 3). Paul's defense of his apostleship, on the other hand, is a convoluted argumentation in continuous style, an impassioned appeal appropriate to the situation of challenge to his authority as the bearer of a novel gospel (see Part III, Section 7).

(*d*) Memory (*mnēmē, memoria*) referred to the process of memorizing the speech so that the delivery would be natural. Various techniques for doing this were devised, the most interesting being the imaginative creation of a scene in which vivid and striking images of persons, objects, and events would be set by association with the points, words, and figures of speech one wished to remember (*Ad Herennium* III.xvi.28—xxiv.40).

(*e*) Delivery (*hypocrisis, pronunciatio*) referred to the use of the voice, pauses, and gestures appropriate to a particular speech occasion. Oratory was carefully distinguished from acting in the theater, even though impersonation was sometimes recommended as a skill appropriate for the realistic description of a situation under review.

2. The Types of Speech

Three "species" of the rhetorical speech were distinguished: the judicial, the deliberative, and the epideictic. Each was thought of as appropriate for the specific occasions of trial before a jury or judge (judicial), political debate within a council or assembly (deliberative), and public occasions of memorial (epideictic). The Greek penchant for classification resulted in a number of additional distinctions, some of which are more helpful than others, but none of which are absolutely definitive. Thus the addition of the category of time created the typology of the judicial issue as past, the deliberative issue as future, and the epideictic issue as present. Looked at from the point of view of the audience, the typology of "judge" for the trial, "critics" for the deliberative speech, and "spectators" for the epideictic speech was sometimes thought to be useful. More telling was the identification of the judicial issue as one of fact and legality (Did he do it or not?), the deliberative issue as one of expediency (Would it be better to do this or that?), and the epideictic issue as turning on the question of honor (What are the grounds for praise or blame?).

Because rhetoric was understood as debate, with two sides to every issue, it was natural for the Greeks to distinguish two contrastive subtypes for each of the three species of speech. These were designated in terms of the overall mode of argumentation that characterized each one. Thus the judicial species consisted of accusation and defense, the deliberative speech of persuasion and dissuasion (later called "confirmation" and "refutation" when applied to the theoretical deliberation of a thesis), and the epideictic of praise or blame. In actual practice, however, a given speech might contain all six forms of argumentation at given junctures, depending on the circumstances. Thus the judicial speech of either accusation or defense regularly called for a section in which the anticipated arguments of the opponent would be refuted. Even though the memorial speech had to attribute honor, and was certainly not the occasion for an opponent's speech in dissent, it might be possible to praise a person's virtues by contrastive innuendos of censure on the opposite kind of behavior. Thus the classifications were heuristic, not definitive. They did, however, establish a general typology for rhetorical performance and had the effect of expanding the use of rhetoric to address an exceptionally wide range of subjects and circumstances. Almost any human occasion could be viewed as debatable and approached rhetorically.

Speech material in the New Testament can be found in each of these three genres. Thus Jesus' instruction on loving one's enemies is cast as a deliberative argument (see Part III, Section 3), the poem to *agapē* in 1 Corinthians 13 is essentially epideictic in form (see Part III, Section 8), and Paul's defense of his apostleship in 1 Corinthians 9 is arranged as a judicial case (see Part III, Section 7). On occasion, it makes some difference whether the argument is to be taken as of this or that type. The recent debate between George Kennedy and Hans-Dieter Betz over the issue in Galatians is a case in point. If the letter is read as an apology (a judicial speech), as Betz holds, the issue involves Paul's own authority and his argument is a defense of his own version of the gospel against other views. If, on the other hand, the letter is deliberative, as Kennedy insists, the issue is not which gospel or whose gospel, but failure by the community addressed fully to live according to a gospel upon which all parties were already in agreement.

Most attempts to define precisely the issue of an early Christian argument fail, however, simply because the social circumstances of the early Christian movements did not correspond to the traditional occasions for each type of speech. Early Christian rhetoric was a distinctively mixed bag in which every form of rhetorical issue and strategy was frequently brought to bear simultaneously in an essentially extravagant persuasion. Thus the occurrence of traditional patterns of argumentation may not always be a firm basis upon which to judge the intention of a speech. Paul's apology, for example, though cast as a judicial issue, obviously intends an epideictic persuasion on his own behalf (see Part III, Section 7). In general, early Christian rhetoric was deliberative in the sense that every aspect of the new persuasion (including the imagination of founder figures and founding events, beliefs, behavior, and the adjudications of social issues) had to be approached as a matter of policy that would determine the future of (membership in) the community.

3. Theory of Argumentation

The rhetors thought about each of the three factors in the communication equation from the point of view of persuasion. The speaker had to be perceived as trustworthy and knowledgeable just to get a hearing. This was discussed under the topic of *ethos* (character). Even if a speaker was not well known to an audience, most rhetors believed that the mode of address itself could establish an acceptable *ethos*. *Ethos* had to be established in the very first part of the speech. Knowing the audience— its convictions, native traditions, and moods—was held to be critical. How to play the audience was discussed under the topic of *pathos* (affection). *Pathos* was especially important toward the conclusion of the speech where heightened style and appeals to emotion and motivation were considered appropriate. Nevertheless, *ethos* and *pathos* always had to be kept in mind throughout the entire speech. It was the content of the speech itself (*logos*), however, that received the greatest attention in the handbooks. *Logos* referred to the ideas, structure, and logic of a speech evaluated in terms of their persuasive force.

Theories of argumentation were devised with both judicial and deliberative (political) issues in mind, but the handbooks reveal that the logic of persuasion was worked out primarily on the model of the judicial speech. Handbooks in the tradition of rhetorical education are generally weak in their discussions of theory, but Aristotle's treatise is clear about the logic of rhetorical argument. That was due to his interest in the difference between rhetorical persuasion and philosophical demonstration (dialectic). Though not taken up into the mainstream until later, Aristotle's treatise can be used to describe what may have been common assumptions from the first, even among those who did not actively pursue philosophical and logical questions. Drawing mainly upon Aristotle, several points can be made about these accepted assumptions of the way in which persuasion worked.

Aristotle's basic point of departure was the recognition that rhetoric engaged issues of social and conventional moment (*nomos*), whereas philosophy aimed at creating conceptual systems within which natural and rational orders could be defined (*physis, cosmos, nous*). As a student of Plato, and thus of Socrates, Aristotle was interested in the nagging question of how to order human society rationally. This question had been posed by the sophists and debated by Plato in terms of a tension between *nomos* (meaning both "law" and "convention") and *physis* (the natural order as perceived by philosophers). Aristotle's treatises on ethics show him at work on this very task and provide the background for his discussions of dialectic and rhetoric in the treatise on rhetoric. When the philosophical theory of reasoning was applied to the logic of persuasion, two points of difference surfaced immediately. One was that the issues engaged by rhetoric were social, contingent, debatable matters focused upon specific events, not things that could be placed in a stable system of hierarchical classification such as the philosophers imagined for the world of reason, nature, and being. The second difference was that, under these circumstances, the most one could argue for was the probability that one way of looking at an issue was better than another. One could not hope to establish truth in the philosophical sense.

These observations led Aristotle to ask about the nature of the data that could be used in rhetorical argument. He recognized that data had to be taken from the legal and cultural traditions of society (*nomos*), and that observations from the natural order of things (*physis*) could at best be used as supporting illustrations. He therefore called a given datum that might be used in an argument a *pistis*, a term scholars now translate as "proof," but which actually meant a commonly shared perspective, persuasion, or belief. Proofs (*pisteis*) were therefore determined by social and cultural convention. Proofs referred to the ways in which people in that society were accustomed to viewing their past and their world. Custom was thus implicitly established as the court of highest appeal in the selection of persuasive arguments (*pisteis*) for a rhetorical argumentation. In arguing a particular case, that is, persuasion would be determined by the degree to which traditional views and values could be marshaled in support of a given case or construction upon it.

A remarkable listing of these traditional views and values was devised. They came to be called the "final topics" or "major aims" (*teleka kephalia*) of the rhetorical speech. A rather consistent listing of these values included eight items, designated in shorthand by using the adjectival form of an abstraction. One might read the list by using the items in the sentence, "If a given proposition can be shown to be (such and such), the argument will hold." The items are: that which is right (*dikaios*), lawful (*nominos*), advantageous (*sympheron*), honorable (*kalos*), pleasant (*hēdus*), easy (*rhadios*), feasible (*dynatos*), and necessary (*anankaios*). Two principles of classification were merged in the making of this list. One was a consideration for the three species of speech, so that the major aims of the judicial (just and lawful), deliberative (advantageous), and epideictic (honorable) might be highlighted. The other principle was to include a graded system for defining a given action under consideration. Later rhetors would rank these in terms of logical and ethical priority. If possible, for instance, it would be better to argue that an action was right, than that it was merely necessary under the circumstances.

One can readily see that the items in this list are empty of specific content, for the level of abstraction excludes any indication of what may have been considered "right" or "lawful" at a given juncture in a social history. This aspect of the theory of rhetoric allowed the practice of rhetoric to survive shifts in cultural orientation. Specific content would have to be supplied by the rhetor, and this meant that a sizable knowledge of social and cultural heritage was absolutely necessary.

Early Christian rhetoric is packed with stock proofs, strategies, and references to the traditional final topics. The trick was to manipulate these in support of their own propositions. By paying careful attention to both expectations given with the traditional patterns of argumentation and the clever accommodations of traditional views and values, the emergence of a substitute set of symbols and values can be discerned in the history of early Christian discourse. One can look at Paul's references to the "law of Christ" (Gal. 6:2 and elsewhere), for instance, not only as a substitute for the Jewish law, but as an accommodation of the Greek notion of *nomos* as well. Social designations were reassigned, as, for instance, with the self-definition intended by the terminologies of *ekklēsia* and kingdom of God. All of the final topics received new nuance in the process, including "what is right," "what is lawful," and "what is good." Early Christians even added their own values to the list of final topics, as is clear from the rhetorical use of the term "blessed" in the Beatitudes and elsewhere. Thus the challenge for early Christians was to (mis)use conventional modes of conviction in the attempt to articulate a new and distinctive ethos.

In order to formulate an argumentation, three logical moves were called for. The first was that a clear position had to be taken with respect to the issue (*stasis*) under review. The position to be taken was variously named, depending upon the type of speech and the history of technical terminology. It might be called the proposition, the thesis, the hypothesis, or the matter (*res*). The second was that a reason for taking the position had to be given immediately, either in the description of the case, or in the form of a syllogism, so that the proposition would be seen as more than a mere assertion. The reason (*ratio*) was frequently called a "cause" (*aitia, causa*) and could form the major premise from which the assertion gained its logical force. The third move was to line up proofs that supported one's contention. The arrangement of these proofs constituted the body of the speech. This was the section called argumentation (elaboration, embellishment, or simply "the proofs"). It is important to have these three moves in mind when analyzing patterns of rhetorical argumentation.

Aristotle wanted to describe rhetorical logic on the model of philosophical (dialectical) reasoning. He had to admit that in comparison with dialectic which preferred deduction from general principles, rhetoric had to argue inductively from maxims or examples taken from social and cultural traditions. He nevertheless suggested that a rhetorical proposition could be formulated deductively by finding a major premise that generalized social and cultural phenomena. He distinguished this kind of syllogism from that used in philosophical reasoning by calling it an *en-*

thymeme (inferred proposition). For Aristotle, the construction of an enthymeme was the basic move involved in formulating a rhetorical thesis.

A New Testament example of an enthymeme is the beatitude, "Blessed are the poor, for theirs is the kingdom" (Matt. 5:3). As was frequently the case in the construction of rhetorical syllogisms, the major premise here was elided. In order for the enthymeme to work, however, the major premise has to be inferable and convincing. In this case the major premise is not questionable: "Those who belong to the kingdom are blessed." The minor premise is given as the reason (*aitia*) in support of the beatitude: "The poor belong to the kingdom." This means that the beatitude itself is actually the conclusion of a rather obvious syllogism (therefore: "The poor are blessed"). The rhetorical advantage of this ploy is gained by inverting the logical process and setting forth the conclusion as if it were a startling pronouncement in need of a supporting argument. Note that if one regards being blessed as a fundamental value in early Christian discourse, which it was, then the syllogism rides on the self-evidence of that value. "Blessed" functions in the place of a standard "final topic," normally used to make an assertion that requires demonstration. In the beatitudes supporting argumentation is not forthcoming. Instead, the notion of blessing is used to list characteristic features of those who belong to the kingdom in the form of an address (to the reader). Later, the reader who has accepted this address will be challenged by a different rhetorical strategy (see Part III, Section 13).

Once the proposition was established, supporting arguments were to be given. Two kinds of supporting arguments (or proof) were regularly distinguished. The first kind of proof was called "nontechnical" (*atechnē*, "uncrafted," sometimes called "external" in modern scholarship), meaning that it did not need to be "invented" by the rhetor. These proofs consisted of laws, precedent decisions, contracts, witnesses, oaths, and the like. (One frequently finds "torture" listed with the nontechnical proofs as well. This referred to the witness of a slave, which was considered valid only if taken under torture; the assumption being that a slave would normally fear to offer testimony against his or her master.) These nontechnical proofs were not at all unimportant, but they were "given," and thus were not thought to challenge the ingenuity of the rhetor as did the invention of strategies, enthymemes, and full-blown argumentations.

In early Christian circles, on the other hand, "nontechnical proofs" were highly prized. The reason seems to be that in the quest for firm foundations both the Jesus movements and the congregations of the Christ imagined events at their beginnings that could establish precedence for subsequent social formations. In order to posit both the occurrence and the significance of these events, narrative description made abundant use of "witnesses," "oracles," "miracles," "oaths," prophetic predictions, scriptural covenants, and the like. All of these were formally classifiable as nontechnical proofs. Naturally, since most of these proofs actually had to be invented, even the marshaling of nontechnical proofs must have been a challenging undertaking for early Christian authors.

In the classical handbooks, major attention was given to the way in which the rhetor's art could put a certain construction upon a case. A large class of invented proofs had to do with strategies by which one might use nontechnical proofs, or other bits of evidence (sometimes called "signs"), or even general considerations (called "probabilities"), to argue for a particular view of a specific event. These strategies actually consisted of elementary forms of logical reasoning. They were often listed as topics and were used to remind the rhetor of the range of options available for crafting a given argument. A short list frequently encountered would include such things as (an argument from) "the opposite," "the same," "the greater," "the lesser." Such designations are not helpful to the modern student unless one sees that they stand for logical procedures. Thus, an argument "from the opposite" meant the use of dialectic reasoning in which some form of the opposite case or circumstance would cinch the positive point. An example would be to argue that it was right to pay taxes by showing that it was wrong not to pay them. The argument "from the lesser" started with a truism about a small or mundane matter in order to say "how much more" it would apply to the "greater" issue at hand. A close reading of early Christian literature will reveal how frequently one encounters arguments based upon strategies such as these.

Yet another classification of proofs was used to describe the kinds of material available to the rhetor other than the material having to do with the nontechnical facts of the case. The generic term for data (in distinction from the strategies) was example (*paradeigma, exemplum*). Three species were regularly listed: the historical example (*paradeigma* proper), the analogy (*parabolē*), and the fable (*mythos*). The difference between the paradigm proper and the other two was that the paradigm was a well-known case taken from history, whereas the analogy and fable were invented, taken not from history but from the worlds of nature and normal social practice. The difference between the analogy and the fable was that the analogy captured a customary observation about types of people, normal events, and regular natural processes, whereas the fable entertained an imaginative world created by fiction. It is extremely important to see that the raw data of rhetorical persuasion consisted of examples, analogies, and fables, and that an example of any kind counted as a proof in a pattern of argumentation, not merely as an illustration in an illuminating instruction.

Early Christians had a great deal of trouble coming up with historical examples because the illustrious examples from either Greek or Jewish tradition clearly exemplified the virtues and values of those cultures and thus were thought inappropriate for early Christian imitation. Since the movements were new, moreover, illustrious examples of Christian behavior were hardly in place to be used as proofs in an argumentation. The early writings are therefore heavily weighted toward the use of analogies. Analogies could be invented and, with some manipulation, could do the work of historical examples as well. This is the case with a large number of analogies with indefinite subjects in the synoptic traditions. References to "the one who . . .," or "a certain person who . . .," or "whoever . . .," frequently serve a pattern of argument in the place of historical examples, inviting the reader to imagine an instance in which the proposition is actualized, even though the instance may be purely hypothetical, imaginary, or idealistic. An example of this usage would be the sayings about "the one who wishes to follow Jesus." There is also a high incidence of class analogies, references to "priests," "workers," "soldiers," and other social roles. In the classical tradition such references would count as analogies from the world of normal practice and behavior, not as examples of particular achievement. In early Christian discourse, however, one notes the tendency toward odd examples, curious applications, and judgmental views on normal practices. Thus the range of analogies extends from natural processes and normal social practices, through peculiar behavior and highly idealistic depictions of unusual performance, to a few carefully selected historical paradigms (e.g., Jesus' obedience unto death). How analogies functioned in a pattern of argumentation should be specified in some detail.

4. The Patterns of Argumentation

The standard form for the rhetorical speech consisted of (1) an introduction (*prooimion, exordium*), (2) a statement of the case (*diēgēsis, narratio*), (3) the supporting arguments (*pistis, confirmatio*), and (4) a conclusion (*epilogos, conclusio*). The introduction acknowledged the situation, addressed the audience, and established the ethos of the speaker. The statement of the case rehearsed the circumstances, clarified the issue (*stasis*), and established the proposition with a reason (*aitia, ratio*) or by appeal to one of the final topics. The argumentation arranged the evidence and supplied examples construed according to customary strategies from the topics. In a judicial speech the argument could also anticipate the proofs of one's opponent and refute them. The conclusion summarized the argument and pressed for its acceptance. It might include impassioned style, exhortation, spelling out the consequences of a decision, or advice.

The standard speech form was developed on the model of the judicial speech. It was easily accommodated to the requirements of the deliberative speech, however, and the deliberative speech was eventually transformed into a standard outline for a "declamation" on a "thesis." At this point, sometime during the second century B.C.E., a simple outline for the development of an argument evolved that was variously called a "thesis," "the complete argument," or an "elaboration." This outline was achieved by naming the major moves of the rhetorical speech in terms of the major types of proof or argumentation. The pattern in effect reduced the complex discussions in the advanced handbooks to manageable size for instructional purposes and it became popular as a guide to rhetorical composition. It consisted of seven or eight items, filling in the four-point outline of the standard speech as follows:

The Standard Speech	The Thesis
I. Exordium	1. Introduction
II. Narratio	2. Proposition
	3. Reason (Rationale)
III. Confirmatio	
	4. Opposite (Contrary)
	5. Analogy (Comparison)
	6. Example
	7. Citation (Authority)
IV. Conclusio	8. Conclusion

This outline for the development of a thesis is an extremely clever combination of formal and substantive designations. Items 2 and 3 explicate the basic requirements of the narratio by calling for a clear statement of the proposition and the reason for its proposal. Together, the proposition and the reason could form what Aristotle called the enthymeme or rhetorical syllogism. In school exercises, however, propositions for theses would be taken from maxims, proverbs, chreiai (anecdotes), citations, as well as stock themes or issues from popular ethical philosophy. It frequently happened, therefore, that the proposition was encoded in figurative language and that the reason was used to decode it by restatement in declarative form.

Item 4 was a shorthand reminder of the fundamental principle that argumentation was debate and that in order to argue a proposition one had to keep the other side of the question constantly in view. How the opposite actually was handled depended upon the type of argument one wished to develop. In a strictly judicial situation, the opposite would have referred to refutation, either of views already proposed by one's opponent, or of opposing views that might be anticipated. In the context of declamation, this item was an opportunity to introduce any contrastive perspective on the proposition that might enhance its plausibility. It was the perfect place for negative contrasts, dissuasions from alternative points of view, charges against those of opposing views, dialectical maneuvers in the interest of verifying the logic of a proposition, censure of the opposite proposition, showing that the opposite case would not make any sense, and so forth. Thus the opposite could be used in a variety of ways, either to enhance the reason for the proposition (and thus function as part of the narratio), or as a first supporting argument that dealt in contrastive analogy (and thus provide a bridge from the narratio to the section on argument).

Items 5 and 6 represent the two major forms of proof or data for constructing the rhetorical argument. Here in the outline for classroom exercises they are positioned as separate items within the section of the speech that amplified or elaborated the proposition by means of supporting arguments. Thus the challenge of the outline was to find ("invent") at least one telling analogy and one apt example in support of the proposition.

Item 7 represents another class of proofs altogether—the nontechnical (or "noninvented"). In a judicial speech this would have referred to some form of witness, precedent legal decision, or documentary evidence. In the elaboration of a thesis, however, this item could be used to cite a philosophical or literary authority as a precedent witness or judgment in favor of the proposition. Thus it is clear that the eight items in this list were carefully chosen to represent in outline the strategies and forms of proof rhetors considered essential for the formation of an argumentation.

Some ingenuity would be necessary to develop even a brief paragraph on this outline. There are examples of school exercises on this model as early as the first centuries B.C.E. and C.E. in the *Ad Herennium* (see 4.43.57) and Theon (see, e.g., the exercise called a "comment" in Hock and O'Neil, 99–101), as well as fine discussions of the thesis exercise in Theon. There is also evidence throughout the literature of the period that this pattern of argumentation became something of a literary convention for the elaboration of maxims and anecdotes, the construction of commentaries, the composition of biographies, and the development of small periods of argumentation even within the genres of wisdom literature and ethical philosophy. In order to see the logic at work, it will be helpful to cite a particularly interesting practice exercise from Hermogenes.

5. The Pattern in Practice

In Hermogenes the pattern is called an elaboration and it occurs in application to a *chreia*. Chreia was the term used by the rhetors to refer to memorable sayings attributed to well-known authorities. Both maxims and crisp rejoinders of the anecdotal variety counted as chreiai. Since chreiai frequently made clever use of figurative language to make their points, teachers of rhetoric saw them as a challenge to logical and argumentative reasoning and used them regularly as theses for the first exercises in rhetorical training. The text cited is from the chapter on the chreia in Hermogenes' *progymnasmata* (Hock and O'Neil, 177). It runs as follows:

But now let us move on to the chief matter, and this is the elaboration. Accordingly, let the elaboration be as follows: (1) First, an encomium, in a few words, for the one who spoke or acted. Then (2) a paraphrase of the chreia itself; then (3) the rationale.

For example, Isocrates said that the root of education is bitter, but its fruit is sweet.

(1) Praise: "Isocrates was wise," and you amplify the subject moderately.

(2) Then the chreia: "He said thus and so," and you are not to express it simply, but rather by amplifying the presentation.

(3) Then the rationale: "For the most important affairs generally succeed because of toil, and once they have succeeded, they bring pleasure."

(4) Then the statement from the opposite: "For ordinary (or chance) affairs do not need toil, and they have an outcome that is entirely without pleasure; but serious affairs have the opposite outcome."

(5) Then the statement from analogy: "For just as it is the lot of farmers to reap their fruits after working with the land, so also is it for those working with words."

(6) Then the statement from example: "Demosthenes, after locking himself in a room and toiling long, later reaped his fruits: wreaths and public acclamations."

(7) It is also possible to argue from the statement by an authority. For example, "Hesiod said:

In front of virtue gods have ordained sweat.

And another poet says:

At the price of toil do the gods sell every good to us."

(8) At the end you are to add an exhortation to the effect that it is necessary to heed the one who has spoken or acted.

At first glance, Hermogenes' exercise appears to be a rather crude stringing together of loosely related items. A closer reading shows, however, that the eight items form a set, that each item was chosen with care, and that the resulting composition forms a period of unified discourse. Each item requires a brief explanation, and the pattern as a whole must be analyzed.

(1) *Praise.* Praise takes the place of the standard introduction because the exercise is exegetical with respect to what Isocrates said and the introduction thus takes on a slightly narrative quality. The student speaker is reporting on the speaker of precedence, not proposing his or her own

thesis. Thus the normal rule for the introduction of a speech (establishment of *ethos*) shifts away from the character of the student speaker to address the character of the speaker who proposed the thesis. This could be done by a brief word of praise, the major objective of the encomium. The logic is the usual, namely that speech and character should match. In this case, the logic works extremely well, for Isocrates was famous as the founder of rhetorical education, the very theme to be drawn from his chreia.

(2) *Chreia.* The chreia is cited or paraphrased as the statement of the case to be argued or the thesis to be defended. It corresponds to the second major division of the standard speech form, the narratio, in which a delineation of the issue comes to climax in a statement of the proposition. In this case the chreia, though aphoristic, states a thesis about the process of education.

(3) *Rationale.* The rationale provides the "reason" why the chreia is true. It also restates the truth of the chreia in a form that can be argued (i.e., as a proposition in need of supporting considerations). To make this move, the student would need to determine the issue embedded within the chreia and find a generally valid proposition that addressed the issue. In this case the issue was discovered in the relationship between the "bitter root" and the "sweet fruit," a relationship left vague by the chreia's metaphoric expression. The proposition interprets the metaphor as a state-ment about the fundamental relationship between "toil" and the success of important affairs. This is more than a restatement of the chreia. It translates the attributes of the metaphor (most probably the vine) into a principle of the necessity of the human activity involved in order to get from the "bitter root" to the "sweet fruit." The rationale plus chreia actually form a rhetorical syllogism in which the rationale serves as the major premise (Important affairs succeed by toil), the minor premise is left unstated (Education is an important affair), and the chreia established as the conclusion to be supported (Hard work at school will bring success).

But the rationale does even more. By translating the "bitter root/ sweet fruit" of the chreia into the sequence "labor first/then rewards," the rationale expressly announces a theme for the elaboration. It also takes the occasion to allude to one of the final topics by suggesting that the eventual success will bring "pleasure" (related to "pleasant," one of the conventional values). This is clever, because a point has already been scored about the success of important affairs being pleasant. If that prop-osition can be sustained in application to education, then its labor will have to be judged worthwhile.

(4) *Opposite.* The logic of the principle proposed is confirmed if the inverse also is true. In this case, a bit of dialectical reasoning was suggested in order to test the validity of the proposition. On the surface of it, this

statement of the opposite is not all that convincing. But in context, the stacking up of connotations with good affairs defined by purpose, toil, and pleasure on the one side, and ordinary affairs defined by happenstance and unhappiness on the other, may have been quite effective.

(5) *Analogy.* By definition the analogy was to be taken from the world of common experience. Analogies were reminders of the way the world worked in general, especially in the spheres of the natural and human orders of activity. They were nonspecific in the sense that the figures indicated were representative and generic types. By referring to a class of persons or objects, or to a regular pattern of occurrence (such as what farmers, doctors, or merchants do), the analogy pointed to a common phenomenon regarded as an instance of a universal principle. The effect of an apt analogy would be the suggestion that the principle stated in the proposition was the same as that implied in the familiar instance. If true of the analogy, then it would be true for the proposition as well.

In this case, the analogy of the farmer is appropriate to the chreia and fits the rules of rhetoric perfectly. The principle of working the land before reaping the harvest can hardly be denied, and the intersection of natural order/human activity means that the analogy has done its work by suggesting universal validity for the proposition. The application to the theme of the elaboration ("working with words") not only explicates the chreia's reference to *paideia* but also serves as a proof that the chreia is true.

(6) *Example.* By definition the example was to be taken from the arena of history. In this case, familiar stories about the famous rhetor were chosen, not only to exemplify the proposition but also to bring the theme of the elaboration home to a specific focus: the proposition of the chreia is particularly true of rhetorical education!

(7) *Citation.* The purpose of the citation was to show that other recognized authorities had come to the same conclusion or rendered a similar judgment on the same issue. In this case a wondrously apt set of citations from Hesiod (289) and Epicharmus (Frag. 287) underscores the necessity of toil, reminds the listener that *paideia* (education) concerns working toward virtue (*paideia*), and grounds the principle of work before harvest in the very order of the gods. All told, the combination of citations from canonical literature with summary theological pronouncements makes a strong climax to this set of arguments.

(8) *Exhortation.* The period is formed by means of an appropriate return to the point of departure. Having demonstrated that what Isocrates said was true, "It is essential to heed him . . ."

The force of the argument as a whole is a result of several designs consciously interwoven. The first is that the unit achieves a measure of aesthetic effect based upon its compositional techniques. Each argument was invented with the chreia as well as the thematic development of the composition in mind. For each item the rhetor returned to the chreia to pick up some aspect of the metaphor still in need of explication. Each item also linked up with the immediately preceding statement in order to develop the chosen theme. Thus there is a sense of new ideas enriching the elaboration as it unfolds. The result is a little paragraph that manifests traits of literary composition.

The second design characteristic is the way in which the final topics were marshaled in the course of the elaboration. None of these values was lifted up expressly in the proposition or in any of the arguments. But several came in for subtle allusion, including the pleasant (in the mention of pleasure), the good (in the mention of "serious affairs," *spoudaios*, and "every good" from the gods), the necessary (in the mention of the "lot" of farmers, the Greek *dei*), the feasible (in the example of Demosthenes), and the right (in the mention of "ordained by the gods"). This was then topped off by the mention of virtue in the citation, constructing an aura of Greek values in support of the proposition.

The third reason for the force of the argument is even more telling and relates to the logic of the outline itself. The design of the outline serves as a chart for investigating all of the orders of human perception, experience, and discourse. Such orders include the arena of logic or dialectic (argument from the opposite), the worlds of nature and human activity (analogy), history and its institutions (example), and literary tradition (citation). That the citations involved references to virtue and the gods may be taken as a fitting complement to this design, since they extend the arenas of discourse to include the fields of philosophy and ethics as well. Taken together, the entire spectrum of social and cultural convention is covered and there is precious little space left upon which to stand in dissent.

Analyzed in this way, it is clear that an elaboration of a chreia, or the development of a thesis, required thought, skill, and ingenuity. At the level of a student's exercise, such an elaboration would have been very demanding. At any subsequent level of authorial achievement, the design would have been capable of challenging even the brightest minds. We shall see that the pattern was put to good use in the several traditions of early Christian argumentation.

6. The Encomium

The epideictic speech followed a somewhat different outline. Its objective was to marshal examples from the life of an individual (or the history of an institution) that could demonstrate the person's virtues and establish the basis for honor or memorial. The speech came to be called an *encomium* and consisted of the following items:

The Encomium
1. Introduction
2. Narration
   Origin/Genealogy/Birth
3. Achievements
   a. Education/Pursuits
   b. Virtues
   c. Deeds
   d. Blessings/Endowments
4. Conclusion
   Honor/Memorial

The encomium pattern was not arranged as an exercise in logical argumentation, following instead a model that was broadly narrative in overall frame but essentially topical in outline. In the section on achievements, however, the encomium made use of examples, a primary form of rhetorical proof. It was also the case that examples of a person's deeds could be enhanced by contrastive images (corresponding to the opposite in a pattern of argumentation), verified by witnesses, illustrated by analogies, and thematized by highlighting one of the final topics as a virtue especially characteristic of the person. Thus the encomium was not devoid of opportunity for using persuasive proofs, although the occasion for an encomium demanded great subtlety lest the rhetor appear to be in need of arguing for a person's honor. It should be emphasized that, in the context of a culture oriented to honor and shame, the attribution of praise was a forceful means of persuasion.

In the New Testament, full-blown encomia are not common, and the notion of virtue as achievement is seriously qualified by a deeply Jewish sensibility, but the use of praise and censure is pervasive nonetheless. Reproach is a critical charge, and woes are customary forms of blame. Praise is frequently its own reward, used to establish *ethos*, undergird *pathos*, create Christian paradigms, and unleash the languages of blessing, thanksgiving, and divine aspiration.

III

Rhetoric in the
New Testament

In this chapter examples of rhetorical composition from the writings of the New Testament will be presented. The examples were selected on the basis of three criteria. First, illustrations were taken from several early Christian movements and traditions. Second, diverse literary genres were chosen in order to illustrate a variety of rhetorical compositions. Third, selection was determined by evidence that a pattern of argumentation had contributed to the arrangement of the composition. In order to see these patterns at work, it is necessary to identify units of argumentation, determine issues and theses, note the nature of the various proofs, and follow the line of thought through to conclusion.

In order to identify a pattern of argumentation, the outlines for the thesis and encomium were used as a guide. It should be emphasized that these outlines were never understood in antiquity as rigid templates, nor has it been assumed here that every rhetorical composition must follow these patterns. The value of the standard patterns is heuristic, providing as they do a checklist of items that frequently occur and a theoretical construct for discerning connections among small units of discourse that might otherwise be overlooked. Few units of composition will unfold in perfect pattern. But the types of material that occur will be the same, the proofs will function similarly, themes will be developed in much the same way, and units will be formed by the same kind of periodizing. The heuristic use of the simple patterns does not frustrate the analysis of rhetorical units that are structured differently. It provides even in these cases a lens for detecting specific rhetorical functions.

The plan will be to identify the major rhetorical functions and proofs of a unit and thus highlight the pattern of argumentation. Rhetorical functions will be identified by using the small list of designations introduced in Part II to outline a pericope or unit of composition. Obviously, these exegetical outlines cannot be thorough even at the point of identifying all of the rhetorical complexities encountered, much less delighting in comprehensive analyses of rhetorical finesse. The purpose of the examples is limited to the demonstration of the fact of rhetorical design on the part of early Christian authors.

One serious problem in the designation of rhetorical functions does need to be acknowledged. The high incidence of analogical material in the New Testament, coupled with the lack of proper examples in early Christian discourse (historical examples, or paradigms proper), means that it is not always easy to assign an analogy to this or that rhetorical function. In general, where different types of analogy occur in the same unit of argumentation, or where a point seems to be made by using analogies from different orders of reality (e.g., nature/social order), the attempt has been made to distinguish the rhetorical functions. One distinction has been to use the term "analogy" for natural order processes, and "example" to identify social order practices. This expands upon the classical definition where "example" usually refers to a specific historical individual, but it seems to be required by the peculiar nature of early Christian rhetoric. The technical term "paradigm" will be used where the classical example (infrequently) occurs.

Illustrations of rhetorical compositions will be taken from the Jesus traditions, the Pauline letters, the Epistle to the Hebrews, and the Gospels and Acts.

A. THE JESUS TRADITIONS

Representative material for the Jesus traditions will be taken from the early layers of Q (the Sayings Source common to Matthew and Luke) and the slightly pre-Markan pronouncement stories. This material is distinctive, for it contains no assumption of kerygmatic or apocalyptic mythology. At this early stage of social history, Jesus' authority was already seen as singular and imperious, but it was not rationalized in terms of a high Christology. His authority was the result of attributing self-referential authorship to him, mainly by means of compounding rhetorical designs. Jesus spoke with authority as the one who elaborated his own pronouncements.

1. Jesus' Teaching on Anxiety: Luke 12:22–31

This is early Q material. It consists of a block of sayings united by the theme of anxiety about food and clothing. Scholars have usually regarded such a block as a cluster of independent, free-floating sayings collected by thematic association. The rhetorical approach looks for a unit of argumentation. The first saying sets the theme in the form of an imperative ("Do not be anxious"). Imperatives are characteristic for early Q, a rhetorical trait that attributes a strong authority to the speaker (*ethos*), and reveals a heightened concern that the audience accept the recommended wisdom as rule (*pathos*). If the imperative is toned down and formulated as a thesis ("One should not be anxious"), a remarkable argumentation can be followed.

An Exhortation Not to Worry

Thesis:	One should not worry about life (food) or body (clothing). (v. 22)
Reason:	Life is more than food, and the body is more than clothing. (v. 23)
Analogy:	Ravens do not work for food; God provides for them. You are worth more than birds. (v. 24)
Example:	No one can add a cubit to life by worry. (v. 25–26)
Analogy:	Lilies do not work, yet are "clothed." (v. 27)
Paradigm:	Solomon was not so arrayed. (v. 27)
Analogy:	Notice the grass that is burned. If God clothes it, how much more will he clothe you? (v. 28)
Conclusion:	You should not seek food (or worry). (v. 29)
Example:	All the nations do that. (v. 30).
Exhortation:	Seek instead the reign of God, and all the rest will be added to you. (v. 31)

Note that the reason constitutes the major premise of a rhetorical syllogism and that the conclusion reiterates the thesis as proven. The minor premise is that God will provide, and it is this that must be argued. Note also that the major premise (reason) is aphoristic, since it is not clear what "more" life may be. This provides the opening for further deliberation. It also provides the topic for a strategy of argumentation called "from the lesser/from the greater." This topic underlies each of the analogies as an argument from the lesser to the greater (people are *more* than natural phenomena). It also occurs in the exhortation as an argument from the greater to the lesser (the reign of God is *more* than all the rest of life).

The argument as a whole is predicated on a theology of nature that guarantees the reign of God. Applied to the human sphere, this theology results in a series of considerations that moves thematically from "worry," through "work," to "seeking," in order to make the switch at the end from what one is not to do (worry), to what one should do (seek the kingdom).

The category of "what is possible" (a final topic) is used in the negative example following the first analogy (it is not possible for anyone to "add a span" of life). All told, the argument is exceptionally tight. It should be noted, however, that it may not have been convincing to any except those who were already socially invested in some discourse about the reign of God.

2. A Controversy about the Sabbath: Mark 2:23–28

This pronouncement story is about plucking grain on the Sabbath. There is scholarly debate about the issue, whether it focuses upon working (plucking) or eating. It is probable that an earlier version of the story was a brief, unelaborated chreia (anecdote) in which the issue was working on the Sabbath, something that was unlawful from the objectors' point of view. The original answer to that objection may have been the rejoinder that "the sabbath was made for people, not people for the sabbath" (v. 27). As it stands, however, the chreia is elaborated as if the objection were to eating on the Sabbath. In either case the issue is judicial. The question is whether the action was a violation of the law. The argument unfolds as a rebuttal to the accusation of illegality:

A Chreia about the Sabbath

Narrative:	Plucking grain on the Sabbath. (v. 23)
Issue:	It is not lawful. (v. 24)
Argument (Rebuttal):	
Citation:	Read the Scriptures. (v. 25)
Example:	What David did (vv. 25–26)
Analogy:	Eating when hungry (v. 25)
Maxim:	Sabbath made for people (v. 27)
Conclusion:	The Son of man is lord even of the Sabbath (v. 28).

Note that the scriptural citation provides several functions at once. It serves as a precedent authority, provides an example, and suggests the analogy of "being in need" because of hunger. The "invention" of this example is clever, because it is taken from the objectors' own literary tradition and used against them. The maxim is also taken from the objectors' store of moral wisdom and states a major premise with which they would have to agree. That the major premise comes at the end is not unusual for an elaborated chreia in the synoptic traditions where the argument regularly concludes with a final authoritative pronouncement. This format gives the impression that the argument unfolded inductively when, as a matter of fact, the elaboration had to be crafted with the pronouncement in mind all along. One sees from this that the construction of a pronouncement story was an exercise in thinking backward, starting with the conclusion and then crafting an inductive approach to it.

In this case the argument is that whereas the Sabbath was made for people, and whereas people need to eat, eating on the Sabbath is not unlawful. This argument is obviously contrived and merely clever, for the objectors would not have said that eating on the Sabbath was unlawful. Note, however, that this line of argument made it possible to introduce the category of need or "what is necessary" (a final topic, v. 25), and that this was taken to justify David's behavior which would otherwise have been unlawful. Even the objectors would have agreed that human need took precedence over "what was lawful" (another final topic), but that argument was hardly the real purpose of the elaboration. By setting up the issue this way, both Jesus and David could be placed on the side of "need" over against the "law." The thought was now possible that just as David was "lord" of the temple (though violating it), so Jesus is "lord" of the Sabbath (though violating it). One sees that the entire argument, the process by which it was contrived, and the mode of reflection revealed by its logic all betray a specific social circumstance as the matrix for the intellectual labor. It is the social circumstance of conflict over Pharisaic codes of ritual purity and the question of their authority for the Jesus movement.

3. Instructions on Loving One's Enemies: Matt. 5:43–48

This is Q material that was reworked by Matthew. Matthew's hand is especially clear in the introduction (v. 43), which is the last of Matthew's six famous antitheses in the Sermon on the Mount ("You have heard. . . . But I say to you"). According to Matthew, loving one's enemies is an example of the righteousness that exceeds that of the scribes and Pharisees (Matt 5:20), whose teaching about love is given by citing Lev. 19:18 ("You shall love your neighbor and hate your enemy"). The instruction about the superior ethic is actually an attempt at deliberative persuasion.

A Thesis on Loving One's Enemies

Thesis:	You should love your enemies and pray for those who persecute you. (v. 44)
Reason:	So that you may be children of your Father in heaven (v. 45a)
Argument:	
Paradigm:	The Father treats just and unjust alike. (v. 45)
Analogy:	The sun rises on both alike.

Analogy:	The rain descends on both alike.
Opposite:	To love one's friends is no distinction. (vv. 46–47)
Example:	Tax collectors (v. 46)
Example:	Gentiles (v. 47)
Conclusion:	Therefore you must be perfect as your Father in heaven is perfect. (v. 48)

Two analogies from the natural order are set over against two examples from the social order to argue for an ethic that surpasses the code given with the scriptural citation. A theology of nature is assumed, as well as the possibility of imitating that divine order. It is not clear that the ethic would have been found attractive on its own merits. The attractiveness of membership in the *ethos* of the movement supports the radical ethic and makes it possible to imagine the argument as convincing. The force of the argument does not reside in its logic, but in its appeal *(pathos)* to imagine the distinction of belonging to a superior ethos.

4. On Wealth and the Kingdom of God: Mark 10:17–31

This material belongs to a section of Mark that is notoriously difficult to parce (Mark 9:38—10:31). The section falls between the second and third prediction units, and appears to serve a function similar to that of the "confession of Peter" (for the first prediction unit) and the transfiguration (for the second prediction unit) by preparing for the prediction and for a set of discipleship sayings to follow. But in this case the material is not narrative, although it is interspersed with several narrative snippits that shift locations and introduce a variety of persons who respond to Jesus' rambling discourse in several ways. The discourse seems to elaborate loosely upon the discipleship sayings in Mark 9:35–37 on greatness in the kingdom, as well as prepare for the final unit on service in the kingdom (Mark 10:32–45). It follows the general theme of entrance into the kingdom, but it does so by interweaving disparate material on following Jesus, rewards, offenses, proper interpretation of the law, children, and wealth. These subthemes pile up and are joined together in the final subsection about wealth.

The unit on wealth is an interesting case of using a chreia as a point of departure for an extended elaboration. An original chreia is discernible in Jesus' first response to the man who called him "Good teacher" (Response: "Why do you call me good?"). This anecdote was elaborated by adding the question about keeping the commandments, the assertion that the man still lacked one thing (selling his possessions in order to follow

Jesus), and the information that the man turned away (and thus forfeited "eternal life"). The elaboration retains the narrative setting, but since the man went away, Jesus can turn to engage the disciples who have been looking on. The argument is deliberative.

Thesis: How to Inherit Eternal Life

Narrative:	A righteous man with great possessions asks about inheriting eternal life. (vv. 17–22)
Issue:	What one should do (v. 17)
Thesis:	One should sell possessions, give to the poor, and follow Jesus. (v. 21)
Reason:	One will have treasure in heaven. (v. 21)
Argument:	
From the Opposite:	
Paradigm:	The man went away sorrowful. (v. 22)
Analogy:	It is easier for a camel to pass through the eye of a needle, than for the wealthy to enter the kingdom of God. (vv. 23–25)
Issue:	Then who can be saved? (v. 26)
For the Thesis:	With God it is possible. (v. 27)
Paradigm:	The disciples have left everything to follow Jesus. (v. 28)
Analogy:	Receiving a hundredfold reward (vv. 29–30)
Conclusion:	
Maxim:	The first will be last, and the last first. (v. 31)

Note that the argumentation finally rests solely on the authority of Jesus to reiterate the thesis. The thesis is supported by means of four arguments. One is a proverb about the first and the last that has been upgraded to the status of a maxim. The second is a theological appeal about all things being possible with God. This is a clever and conscious misuse of the category "what is possible" (a final topic). In Greek parlance, this category referred to what was humanly possible; here it has been used of the divine order set in contrast to the human. This consideration undergirds the third argument in support of the thesis, namely, the force of contrastive examples. The man did not, the disciples did find it "possible" to leave all and follow Jesus. The fourth argument is the analogy of the camel. It is the only argument taken from the realm of common sense, and is used to mediate the opposition between possible and impossible by substituting the categories of "easy" and "difficult" (also taken from the traditional list of final topics). The sense of the whole is that, though it is difficult to follow Jesus, it is possible and, in light of the heavenly rewards, worth it. Again, though the form of the argument follows standard conventions, its force must derive from the attractiveness of the social ethos it assumes, not from the logic of the argument itself.

B. THE PAULINE TRADITION

Turning from the Gospels to the letters of Paul, a very different rhetoric is encountered. Paul's letters are a window into the congregations of the Christ where the fundamental persuasion was kerygmatic. In this context, the authority of the apostle was a burning issue, not the authority of Jesus as a founder-teacher.

5. Belief in the Resurrection: I Cor. 15:1–58

Paul's famous chapter on the resurrection of the dead is a perfect example of rhetorical argumentation. It follows the short outline of a thesis elaboration by moving from thesis, to reason, contrast, example, analogy, citation, and conclusion. Because the thesis is partly philosophical, partly an issue of fact, however, strategies from judicial modes of argumentation are interwoven into an essentially deliberative declamation. One example of this is that considerable effort is given to defining the issue of fact. Another is that each major section except the conclusion is constructed not only to state the positive point but also to counter questions that might easily be raised to refute his contentions. This touch of forensic strategy makes the argument weighty. By overlooking for the moment these second-level considerations, the basic pattern is easily discerned.

Thesis: There Will Be a Resurrection

Exordium:	Address to the Corinthians with reminder of their reception of the gospel (vv. 1–2)
Narratio:	How the preaching of the kerygma, including the resurrection of Christ, came to the Corinthians (vv. 3–11)
Issue:	Some say that there is no resurrection of the dead. (vv. 12–19)
Fact:	In fact Christ was raised from the dead,
Thesis:	the first fruits of those who have died. (v. 20)
Argument:	
Paradigms:	Just as Adam brought death, so Christ brought life. (vv. 21–28)
Opposite:	Each in his own order
Examples:	Baptizing for the dead
	Dying daily for the gospel
	Fighting beasts at Ephesus (vv. 29–34)

Analogies:	Seed that dies and comes to life
	Different kinds of body (vv. 35–44)
Citation:	The Genesis account of the creation of Adam,
	a "living being," from the dust (vv. 45–50)
Conclusion:	A narrative description of the eschatological
	resurrection of the dead, a scriptural citation,
	a thanksgiving, and an exhortation (vv. 51–58)

The issue concerns the resurrection "of the dead," not of the Christ. Paul uses this difference to great advantage by starting with the observation that if there is no resurrection of the dead, then Christ (also) has not been raised (v. 13). This sets him up for his argumentation which, however, actually works the other way around, from the kerygma to the resurrection of the dead. In order to make sure that the kerygma does not come into question, Paul unfolds a series of consequences in the form of a *sorites* (interlocking chain):

If Christ is not raised, then preaching is in vain.
If preaching is vain, then your faith is vain.
If faith is vain, then you are yet in your sins.
If sin is still victor, then the dead have perished.
If that is the case, then we are to be pitied.

This ends on a pathetic note, showing that Paul's argument was designed not to give reasons for the trustworthiness of the kergyma but to ward off questions about it. Interspersed is one other consideration of the same kind, an insinuation of being guilty of false witness before God if in fact God did not raise Jesus as the apostles have testified.

In the section on the reason, with its comparison and contrast between Adam and Christ as corporate symbols, the conceptual problem is even more serious. In order to make the application to the issue of the dead, Paul has to project a future time ("shall be made alive"). He wards off the question this might raise about logical consistency by introducing another *sorites*, this one consisting of a series of eschatological events in order. It includes the resurrection of the dead, then goes on to celebrate the victory of Christ and the kingdom over all enemies, finally to culminate in a grand subjection of everything to God. If the preceding *pathos* was avoidance of being pitiful, this appeal is clearly to a sense of exuberant vindication.

The section of examples is the weakest link in the argumentation. Why Paul put himself in peril, or why people baptized on behalf of the dead, are better questions than proofs. In order to make them appear as important examples in support of the resurrection faith, Paul immediately introduced the contrast of others who eat, drink, and are merry. He even found (invented) a proverb from Menander, "Bad company ruins good morals," insinuating that the Corinthians needed this advice, and ended by imputing their shame. This is clearly another example of Paul's use of *pathos* to bolster a weak argument.

The analogy of the seed works somewhat better, for the metaphor of sowing was familiar in educational discourse. The problem was that it also did not exactly fit the issue of resurrection. In order to make it fit, Paul introduced the notion of plural kinds of seeds and bodies, then pressed the distinction between earthly and heavenly bodies, in order to arrive at the image of sowing the physical body and raising a spiritual body. Paul apparently thought that this argument was his strongest, for he states succinctly in conclusion, "If there is a physical body, there is also a spiritual body."

The citation from Genesis on the creation of Adam follows nicely, for the story tells of the man of dust becoming a living being. The problem in this case, however, is twofold. The analogy works no better than that of the seed, for the living being is not a resurrected body. And besides, Paul had already referred to Adam (in the reason for the thesis) as the one who brought death, not life, upon all. Paul anticipates these embarrassing queries by immediately introducing (again) the need for sequential arrangement. First is the physical, then the spiritual; first the man from the earth, then the man from heaven; first the bearing of the Adam image, then the bearing of the Christ image. The incremental shifts eventuate in the pronouncement, "Flesh and blood cannot inherit the kingdom of God, nor does the perishable inherit the imperishable." That seems to be the clincher, after which Paul concludes with a positive apocalyptic prediction and an exhortation to stand fast "knowing that your labor in the Lord is not in vain."

Note that the argument is not designed to support the first half of the thesis ("in fact Christ has been raised from the dead"), but the second ("the first fruits of those who have fallen asleep"). This means that the kerygma is not only the point of departure for, but the ultimate ground of Paul's persuasion. None of the arguments are introduced in support of the kerygma, but in support of Paul's contention that the kergyma guarantees the resurrection of the dead. Thus the kerygma functioned for Paul and his congregations as a presupposition for further theological thinking in the same way that the cultural traditions of Greeks and Jews served as conventions from which arguments could be drawn.

Note also that the apocalyptic persuasion is introduced in order to explicate the significance of the kerygma for the resurrection of the dead; it is not derived from the kerygmatic persuasion itself. This is a rhetorical observation that may have great significance for the reconstruction of early

Christianity and its faith, indicating as it does that the apocalyptic persuasion may have been a second-level development, not basic to the process by which the kerygma was imagined in the first place.

6. Paul's Appeal for the Collection: 2 Corinthians 9

This chapter is addressed to the Achaians and contains Paul's exhortation for a collection of gifts in support of the pious poor in Jerusalem. The exhortation generally follows the standard outline for deliberation, except that after the argument in support of the thesis (that the Achaians should contribute to the collection), Paul takes full advantage of the conclusion to advance another set of arguments. These arguments are not formulated as syllogistic support for the thesis, but as pathetic appeals to encomiastic ideals. This does not violate the rhetor's privilege, for the conclusion of any speech was the proper place for pathetic appeal, but the shift in type of argument does make it more difficult to follow the line of reasoning. In the first section, the argument is that one will be rewarded. In the second, the appeal is to honor. By treating the conclusion of the argumentation in v. 10 as the subtle introduction of a new encomiastic theme or thesis, the link can be seen that joins the two major sections of this exhortation.

An Exhortation to Contribute

Exordium:	Address to the audience with praise for their earlier promise and readiness to contribute (vv. 1–2)
Narratio:	Paul sends the letter and the brothers in advance to make sure that when he arrives with the Macedonians, he will not be humiliated and the Achaians will not be forced by shame into keeping a promise as yet unfulfilled. (vv. 3–5)
Thesis:	Generous giving will be rewarded. (Implied, v. 6)
The Arguments:	(vv. 6–10)
Analogy:	Sowing and reaping (v. 6)
Proverb:	God loves a cheerful giver. (LXX Prov. 22:8; v. 7)
Pronouncement:	God is able to provide in abundance. (v. 8)
Citation:	"God scatters, gives to the poor; his righteousness endures." (Ps. 112:9; v. 9)
Conclusion:	God will supply the seed, multiply the sowing, and increase the harvest, both of physical resources and of "your righteousness." (vv. 10–11a)
The Exhortation:	(vv. 11–14)

Honor:	The challenge is a test of faith and obedience to the gospel.
Virtue:	Passing the test will demonstrate the virtues of faith, obedience, generosity, piety, and grace.
Reward:	Others will recognize your Christian virtue, pray for you, and give thanks to God.
Conclusion:	Thanks be to God. (v. 15)

The argument is based upon a natural theology that gains its force by merging Jewish wisdom with a Greek commonplace about sowing and reaping. The Psalm citation (that mentions "scattering," "the poor," and "righteousness") cleverly introduces the notion of piety (righteousness) and treats it mimetically ("your righteousness"). This makes it possible to interpret the reward for sowing in terms of the harvest of recognition for manifesting Christian virtues. The exhortation that follows is epideictic rhetoric in its appeal to honor (the final topic of epideictic) versus shame (cf. 9:4). The virtues, however, are carefully described as signs of Christian piety (obedience to the gospel), not to be confused with Jewish or Greek piety and ethic. One nevertheless discerns other standard final topics (what is right, lawful, advantageous, honorable, pleasant, feasible, and necessary) lurking beneath the surface of their Christian transformations. This process of domestication created some difficulties, however, mainly because the Greek definition of honor was based on human achievement and that really did not fit Paul's understanding of Christian virtue that was based on faith in the achievements of God. Note the slippage therefore in Paul's appeal. The service of the Achaians will result in glory to God, and the recognition of their honor will result in others giving thanks to God. Thus the rhetorical analysis captures a poignant moment in the self-definition of early Christianity as it carves out a distinctive ethos in contrast to the larger cultures of context.

7. Paul's Defense of His Apostleship: 1 Corinthians 9

Paul announces his defense *(apologia)* in v. 3. This indicates a judicial issue and assumes that some charge has been made against him. The charge is not given, but the nature of his defense indicates that it had to do with his failure to demand payment for his services. This can be understood against the general practice of teachers and rhetors accepting fees for their instructions. The charge against Paul may have been nothing more than a scurrilous remark about his free advice with the innuendo that it was not worth any more than that. It certainly was not a serious legal accusation, as if Paul had broken some law. Paul's defense was therefore a judicial ruse. The real issue was the status of his authority as an apostle. Paul nevertheless used the ploy of defending himself in court, using the customary questions for the determination of an issue to great epideictic advantage. The customary questions were questions of (1) fact (Did he or did he not do it?), (2) legality (What law comes in question?), (3) definition (Was it murder, manslaughter, self-defense, etc.?), and (4) quality (motivation). Because the issue is really epideictic (concerning Paul's authority and honor as an apostle), the reader needs to catch the ethical nuance to every legal question that occurs.

Paul's Defense

Exordium: Paul's introduction of himself as an apostle to the Corinthians despite what others may say about him (vv. 1–2); his defense before those who would examine him (v. 3) will be as follows:

A Partition of the Facts of the Case:

First Question (of law): What is the law?

    Thesis: An apostle has the right to support. (v. 4)

    Arguments:

      Paradigms: The apostles, the brothers of the Lord, Cephas. (vv. 5–6)

      Examples: Soldiers, Vinters, Herdsmen. (v. 7)

      Legal Citation: Moses' law: Do not muzzle the ox. (Deut. 25:4; vv. 8–9)

      Interpretation: Both the "plowman" and the "thresher" hope for a share of the crop. (v. 10)

Application to the case of Paul and Barnabas:

      Comparison: If others have a right to your material benefits, how much more we. (vv. 11–12)

      Example: Temple servants get their food. (v. 13)

      Example: Temple priests share in the offerings. (v. 13)

      Law: The Lord commanded that those who preach the gospel should get their living by the gospel. (v. 14)

    Conclusion: (Implied: Paul has the right.)

Second Question (of Fact): Did Paul accept support?

    Statement of admission: No, he did not.

      Reason: In order not to place an obstacle before the gospel (v. 12)

    Conclusion: Thus Paul has grounds for boasting. (v. 15)

    (This leads to questions of the definition and quality of the act.)

Third Question (of Definition): What exactly did Paul do?

    Thesis 1: Paul had to preach the gospel.

      Reason: Because he was commissioned

Thesis 2:	He did not have to charge.
Proof:	He willingly relinquished his rights.
Conclusion:	That Paul did not charge for his preaching is therefore a ground for boasting or reward. (vv. 16–17)

Fourth Question (of Quality): Why did Paul do that?

Assertion:	To make the gospel free of charge and to win more converts. (v. 18)
Example:	Voluntarily becoming a slave to others (vv. 19–22, 11)
Assertion:	To share for himself in the blessings of the gospel.
Example:	Athletes running for a prize (vv. 23–27)

Paul's strategy involved making two critical moves. One was to separate the question about fees from the question about the value of his preaching. He achieved this by means of a shrewd use of the stock questions for determining the exact issue in a judicial trial. Preaching the gospel was a matter of necessity (a standard final topic), but charging fees was a voluntary matter (another standard topic). This move cut to the heart of the criticism, leaving the value of the gospel untouched by the fee question, and leaving Paul free to put a positive construction on both his preaching of the gospel and his "failure" in the matter of receiving support.

The second critical move was made possible by the ruse of legal analysis. Note that Paul spent a great deal of effort to argue for the legal right of the preacher to be supported. This was no doubt a novel notion, but may have been thinkable simply because practices of support were already in place, if not such a rationale. The rationale was achieved primarily by linking a (farfetched) "law of Moses" (vv. 8–10) with the "command" of the Lord (v. 14; cf. Luke 10:7), but its persuasive force must have lain in the large number of analogies and examples used to demonstrate the principle. Beneath it all is the idea of making a living, especially earning one's food, instead of the idea of fees. This allowed Paul to use the stock metaphor of sowing and reaping which occurs throughout, and to shift the subject from support (reaping) to his work of sowing the (spiritual) seed of the gospel (v. 11). By going out of his way to agree with his critics on the right of the preacher to reap benefits from his labor, Paul could capitalize on his voluntary deprivation as noble and self-sacrificial behavior.

Thus Paul turned a criticism to positive advantage. His behavior could now be seen as absolutely commendable. By not charging for the gospel, he practiced what he preached (*imitatio Christi*), set the gospel free, engaged others as a servant, and could hope that he also might share finally in the (spiritual) rewards of the gospel (salvation as an "imperishable wreath"). But that is not all!

The real issue had to do with Paul's authority as an apostle. This is clear from the exordium: "Am I not free? Am I not an apostle? Have I not seen Jesus our Lord? Are you not my workmanship in the Lord?" Reading the defense with these rhetorical questions in mind, the marvelous tour de force comes clear. The real points were made subtly and had nothing to do with the judicial exercise. They had rather to do with the "law of Christ" (v. 21). Read against the background of Galatians, and in the light of 1 Cor. 15:3–11, Paul managed to write his own encomium as an apostle, commissioned (by the Lord), free (from human tradition), and obedient to the mission. If one were to arrange Paul's profile according to the encomium outline, then all of the major categories would be addressed:

An Encomium on Paul

Birth:	Free, not a slave (vv. 1, 19, 22–23)
Education:	Commissioned (v. 17)
Virtues:	Wisdom (v. 11), endurance (v. 12), courage (v. 15), philanthropic (vv. 19–23), disciplined (vv. 26–27), etc.
Manner of Life:	Sacrificial, consistent with the law of Christ
Deeds:	Preaching, labors
Achievements:	Converts, winning more
Rewards:	An imperishable wreath

Such a rhetorical analysis may be helpful for the task of sorting through the issues of authority that faced early Christian communities and leaders, and for the task of sorting out less important arguments to get at the fundamental persuasions that energized the new movement. In this case, Paul's own point of departure and court of final appeal was his experience and understanding of the gospel. Even if others held different opinions about Paul and his interpretation of the gospel, the rhetoric could have worked only if his audience was also involved in a social adventure that was seeking its grounding in some message about Jesus as a founder figure. At stake, however, is the authority of the messenger as well as the particular content and consequence of the message.

Note that Paul's understanding of his apostleship is no different here from that expressed in Galatians; nevertheless, his claim to special revelation, emphasized in Galatians, does not surface here as a point essential to his argumentation. Instead, the argument is based on the agreement of the two laws, that of Moses and that of Jesus. This is not strange per se, for the logic of persuasion always seeks to marshal tradition in support of a contention. But it is strange in the context of Paul's otherwise adamant insistence on the novelty of the gospel (against the background of the Jewish law), and that its content is the word of the cross (not a "command of the Lord"). Thus the rhetorical analysis has identified a most unusual rhetorical situation, a situation in which Paul appealed to authorities not basic to his theology. This finding might help determine more precisely just who it was that Paul was trying to impress, and why.

8. The Encomium on Agape: I Corinthians 13

This well-known chapter has usually been called a hymn to love, understood as a divine Christian grace. It is actually an encomium on one of the human affections that came to be seen as virtues during the Greco-Roman period. Others were trust (*pistis*), hope (*elpis*), and patience (*hypomonē*). Hellenistic Jews such as Philo of Alexandria treated these affections in the same way that they treated the virtues traditional with the Greeks (righteousness, wisdom, courage, prudence, and others). Those virtues thought to be more significant, such as wisdom or rightness (*dikē, dikaiosynē*), were frequently personified as forces that made (or should make) a difference in the way the world was ordered and the way history worked out. The quasi personification turned these human affections into ideals that came back to haunt the average creature as fantastic challenges. Many of these abstract Hellenistic virtues occur in this encomium in slightly mythological dress. It was not unusual for encomia to be written on virtues such as these and other noble conceptions. This one on *agapē* (a term readily translated as "affection," with connotations of "regard," "respect," and "fondness") is enhanced by a heightened poetic style, a studied use of terminology, and a careful thematic organization. Scholars have sometimes called this type of composition a prose hymn, thus justifying the traditional designation.

The encomium fits uneasily in the context of an argument about the leadership gifts of preaching, prophecy, "tongues," healing, and so forth. It is introduced as a "more excellent way," that is, a way of life, or ethic. But at the end, Paul's discussion resumes by urging the Corinthians to "desire eagerly the spiritual gifts, especially prophecy." It is therefore not clear that the encomium has been given its due, for its point is just the emptiness or even harmfulness of such gifts in comparison with the virtues of faith, hope, and *agapē*. It does appear that some Christian poet drew upon popular religious philosophy in order to counter the extravagant claims of spiritual entrepreneurs to special powers and authority, exactly the issue Paul was addressing. Paul made use of the poem for his own purposes, of course, to argue that spiritual gifts should be used to edify the community. But this hardly does justice to the poem which offers a much more radical critique of just such charismatic activity.

In Praise of Agape

1. **Definition:**	Agape is all that counts. (vv. 1–3)
Contrast:	Speaking without agape is noise. (v. 1)
Example:	Sublime oratory
Analogy:	Music
Contrast:	Esoteric knowledge without agape is nothing. (v. 2)
Examples:	Prophetic gifts
	Total knowledge
	Effective faith
Contrast:	Extravagant gifts without affection gain nothing. (v. 3)
Examples:	Giving away all one's possessions
	Giving one's life as a martyr
2. **The Virtues:**	Agape endures everything. (vv. 4–7)
a) Qualities:	Patience and kindness
Opposites:	Jealousy, boastfulness
	Arrogance, rudeness
b) Actions:	Agape does not insist on its own way.
Examples:	Neither irritable, nor resentful
Contrast:	Does not rejoice in violation of justice; does rejoice in the truth.
c) Achievements:	Agape masters every eventuality.
Examples:	Sustains all things
	Entrusts all things
	Hopes utterly
	Endures everything
3. **Rewards:**	
a) Success:	Agape will never fail. (vv. 8–13)
Opposites:	Prophecies will be rendered useless.
	Languages will cease.
	Knowledge will be rendered useless. (v. 8)
Reason.	Human knowledge and prophecy are imperfect. (v. 9)
b) Recognition:	The partial will be rendered useless when the perfect arrives. (v. 10)
Example:	Childlike speaking, understanding, and reasoning is left behind when becoming an adult. (v. 11)

Analogy:	A dim reflection versus face-to-face encounter (v. 12)
4. **Memorial:**	Only three gifts will last: Faith, hope, and agape. Agape is the greater of the three. (v. 13)

Agapē is eulogized as a victorious stance toward any and all eventualities. The contrast seems to be a desire to effect change in others or to control circumstances. A comprehensive typology of human actions illustrates the danger of using speech, knowledge, fidelity, and even voluntary sacrifice without agape. The contrasts to *agapē* that occur in each of the three sections of the encomium are probably to be taken together, for thematic development is not lacking. Note, for instance, that the transitions are smooth, picking up on the previous concept and expanding upon its connotation to move the subject ahead. Thus prophecy in v. 2 combines speaking (v. 1) and special knowledge (v. 3), martyrdom in v. 3 combines giving up (the previous action) and endurance (the theme of the next section), endurance in the section on the virtues leads easily into the subject of endurance in the section on lasting forever, and so forth. The negative virtues of boasting, jealousy, arrogance, and rudeness in the middle section correspond to the critique of prophetic activity and the display of special powers in sections 1 and 3. Thus the argument is indirect. It gains its force only because of the honor/shame opposition basic to the encomium.

The encomium, for its part, is persuasive mainly because of its poetic enchantments, not because of its logic. *Agapē* is defined only by negative contrasts and passive qualities. The two expressly supportive arguments (child/man and mirror/presence) are not enough to feel confident about the point of agape's perfection. And the final statement about *agapē* being greater than faith and hope is neither supported nor developed. The only telling description of the perfection in mind is the author's aside in v. 12 about "fully understanding even as I have been fully understood." This, however, scuttles the entire program, for it substitutes a private desire for the otherwise potentially ethical considerations. Perhaps this fatal flaw in the argumentation was the reason for Paul's cool approach.

9. Paul's Letter to the Galatians

This letter has often been used to illustrate Pauline rhetoric because it clearly addresses an issue of social and ideological conflict, and because it is so polemical, argumentative, and exhortative in tone. The precise issue, however, is still a matter of scholarly debate, and the argument is very difficult to follow. Even Betz, whose commentary on Galatians is organized rhetorically, and Kennedy, whose special expertise is classical rhetoric, disagree on the issue and outline of argument for Galatians. Betz holds that the letter is a defense of Paul's gospel, and that the proposition of Paul's gospel is that justification comes by faith, not by works of the law. Kennedy notes that the six arguments identified by Betz in the body of the letter do not evenly work in support of that proposition, and that the repeated exhortations indicate a deliberative, not a judicial, intention. Kennedy thinks that the purpose is simply to persuade the Galatians not to fall back into Judaism, but to continue in the Christian faith.

This disagreement is enlightening, for each scholar has seen clearly that rhetorical technique is at work in the letter, that Paul is concerned about the Galatians falling away from his gospel of freedom, and that the argument combines close reasoning on law and gospel, as well as exhortation to Christian freedom. The disagreement, then, is whether the letter corresponds to this or that species of rhetorical speech, and whether a unit of argumentation can be clearly designated in terms of a single speech function. It is not unimportant to determine the issue at stake in an argument. But in this case, the search for a single issue, single thesis, and single mode of rhetoric overlooks the complex situation Paul addressed and the tortured path of his reasoning.

The situation was that the Galatians had entertained "another gospel" between the time of Paul's mission among them and the occasion for the letter (1:6). The other gospel recommended circumcision and, as it appears, the keeping of Jewish ritual occasions as proper responses to their having become members of Israel (2:7–8, 12; 4:10; 5:2–12; 6:12–15). Paul was enraged, suspecting that the views of the "circumcision party" from the pillars at Jerusalem had been introduced. It was now his gospel, a gospel that did not require Gentiles to be circumcised, against that other gospel. Paul's authority as an apostle also came into question. Since Paul obviously thought that the Galatians were still amenable to persuasion, one has to imagine them as divided or at least uncertain about the matter. Thus Paul's letter had to address at least three audiences or perspectives on the issue: Gentile converts of Paul, Jewish Christians of conservative persuasion, and those Gentiles who were entertaining the thought of becoming circumcised and keeping other conventions of the Jewish law.

The issue, moreover, could be phrased in a variety of ways. Refuting the assumptions of the other gospel would be one way. Showing that his gospel was enough, that it did not require the addition of circumcision, would be another. Clearly establishing his credentials to know what the gospel for Gentiles should be would be yet another. A fourth would be the expressly deliberative issue of exhorting the Galatians not to give away the precious spirit that defined their gatherings before the troublermakers ever arrived. Paul actually forged all four issues into a single letter of passion and persuasion, theoretical construction and devastating refutation.

The argument can be followed, but with difficulty, for shifts among the issues take place, arguments appear ad hoc and out of logical sequence—arguments that frequently assume Paul's understanding of the kerygma without explication. Refutations also occur all mixed up with the constructive proposals. Pieces of exordium and exhortation are even interspersed throughout the letter, and each is taken as an occasion for making additional arguments, not left merely as address and concluding appeal. The letter unfolds, nonetheless, essentially on the pattern of a rhetorical speech. Standard topics (such as enthymemes, greater/lesser, earlier/later, honor/shame) and arguments (such as examples, analogies, maxims, and citations from Scripture) are used throughout. Thematic development also occurs, especially in the case of the ideas of spirit, sonship, and freedom. Thus the rhetorical techniques can be identified and the argumentation assessed.

Two strategies are crucial for Paul's construction, and they must be understood in order to make any sense at all of his argument. The first is that his treatment of the Scriptures distinguishes among "law," "oracle," and "epic." Such distinctions were not a novelty with Paul, but the way in which he ranked them may have been his own doing, and the way in which he used them to support his argument about the gospel is clearly without precedent. While the Scripture as oracle counts as an authoritative statement of truth, and the Torah as epic counts as precedent etiology for Christianity, the Scripture as law is a negative entity to be rejected. The situation demanded that Paul address the question of the law in relation to his claim that the God of Israel had welcomed and "justified"Gentile Christians. He did so by treating the Mosaic law as a temporary and inadequate covenant.

The other significant strategy is the way the epic was treated. The basic move was to bracket the period of the law and establish a positive correlation between Abraham, the father of Israel, and Christ, the founder of Christianity. Formally, this corresponds to a common strategy in myth-making where an earlier period is idealized, then used to criticize the recent past held to be decadent. But Paul's choice of Abraham (instead of Moses) as the definitive founder figure for Israel, and his thorough elaboration of this epic rationale for Christian freedom from the law, appears to be a marvelously idiosyncratic achievement. He did this in order to cancel out any claim that the Mosaic law might be said to have upon Gentile Christians.

The decision to base his argument on such an epic rationale affected the way the argument could unfold. The epic argument is narrative in form, while the patterns of rhetorical persuasion are topical and thematic. Since both forms of argumentation are merged in Galatians, the flow of discourse is decidedly bumpy, segmented, and circular. Themes give way to points about the epic sequence, then both are sprung by units of syllogistic logic or the elaboration of an analogy. In order to chart the major moves in sequence, a set of headings will be used that merge epistolary, rhetorical, narrative, and thematic categories of organization. The result is a rather complex outline, but one that should be recognizable as having a rhetorical design. There are five units of argumentation in the main body of the letter. These five units have in common the desire to define Christians as the true children of Abraham. This means that the issue overall is cast in terms of judicial definition: Who is worthy to receive the inheritance of that divine promise to Abraham? Each of the five units sets forth a subthesis on this theme and develops its own pattern of supporting argumentation.

Thesis: The True Children of Abraham

Epistolary prescript (1:1–5)

> Paul is an apostle of Christ.
>
> The Galatian churches are reminded of the gospel.

Exordium (1:6–10)

> Paul's astonishment: Another gospel is being preached in Galatia. Curses on those who preach it. See: Paul does not say things just to please.

Narratio (1:11—2:14)

> Paul's gospel was received by special revelation.
>
> Paul's revelation included a commission to Gentiles.
>
> Agreement was reached with the other apostles:
>
>> At the belated conference in Jerusalem, Paul's gospel was accepted by the pillars. Paul's gospel was to the Gentiles who did not need to be circumcised. Peter's gospel was to the Jews (the circumcised).
>
> Conflict at Antioch:
>
>> Paul withstood Peter. The circumcision party had intimidated Peter and Barnabas; they withdrew from table fellowship with Gentiles.

Issues and Thesis (2:14–3:5)

> Paul's question to Peter:
>
>> If you, a Jew, live like a Gentile, how can you compel Gentiles to live like Jews?
>
> Paul's gospel:

Both Jews and Greeks are justified by faith in Christ, not by works of the law.

Paul's question to the Galatians:

O foolish Galatians, having started with the spirit, will you now end up in the flesh?

Major Thesis:

The Galatians are true children of Abraham because of their faith in Christ. They do not need to be circumcised and keep the Jewish law in order to receive the promise of the spirit.

Argumentation:

The Oracle as Contract is Assumed:

A. God made a promise to Abraham and his children.

B. This promise remains in force.

I. Definition: The true children of Abraham (3:6–9)

A. Enthymeme: Abraham's faith and righteousness

Major Premise (implied): God made a promise to Israel.

Minor Premise (citation): "Abraham believed God and it was reckoned to him as righteousness." (Gen. 15:6)

Conclusion: Those of faith are the (true) children of Abraham.

B. Enthymeme: Those included in the blessing

Major Premise (implied): Abraham was blessed for his faith.

Minor premise (citation): "In you shall all the nations be blessed." (Gen 12:3; 18:18)

Conclusion: The Gentiles of faith are blessed with Abraham.

II. The Question of Claim Based on Law (3:10–12)

Proposition: Those who rely on the law are cursed.

Citation: "Cursed is every one who does not abide by all things written in the book of the law, and do them." (Deut. 27:26)

Reason 1: The law justifies no one.

Citation: "He who through faith is righteous shall live." (Hab. 2:4)

Reason 2: The law does not rest on faith (but works).

Citation: "He who does them shall live by them." (Lev. 18:8)

III. The Question of Redemption (3:13–16)

A. Fact and Quality: Christ died under the law to redeem from the curse of the law.

Citation: "Cursed be every one who hangs upon a tree." (Deut. 21:23)

Kerygma: Having become a curse "for us"

B. Consequence: Through Christ the promise to Abraham passes to the Gentiles.

Major Premise: The promise was made to Abraham and to his offspring.

Minor Premise: Christ is the offspring (seed) of Abraham.

Reason (citation): "Offspring" is singular, not plural.

Conclusion: The promise of the blessing is "in Christ."

IV. The Question of Jurisdiction: Law or Promise (3:15, 17–24)

  A. The law cannot annul the promise.

    Example: ratification of wills

    Topic (prior/subsequent): The law came 430 years later.

  B. The law was added for other reasons.

    It was added because of transgressions.

      Citation: The Scripture consigned all things to sin.

    It was a temporary mediation.

      Reason: Angel myth

    It could not make alive.

      Reason: If so, righteousness would have come by the law.

    It served as constraint until Christ.

      Examples: Pedagogues; guardians; trustees

    Conclusion: The inheritance is based on promise, not on law.

V. Conclusion: The inheritance is available to Gentile Christians (3:25—4:7)

  Proposition: In Christ you are all children of God through faith.

    Example: Baptism

      Major premise: Christ is Abraham's offspring.

      Minor premise: Baptism into Christ means belonging to Christ.

        Analogy: "Putting on" Christ

        Assertion: You are all "one" in Christ. "There is neither Jew nor Greek, slave nor free, male nor female."

      Conclusion: If you are Christ's, then you are Abraham's offspring, heirs according to promise.

    Example: Heirs receiving the inheritance.

    Example: Slaves receiving adoption.

    Paradigm: God sent his Son to redeem those under the law.

    Witness: "Abba Father" is the cry of the spirit of God's Son sent into our hearts.

    Conclusion: "Through God you are no longer a slave, but a son, and if a son then an heir."

Exhortation (4:8–20): Don't fall back into enslavement to the elemental spirits.

    Remember when I preached the gospel to you at first.

    Beware those who are now solicitous of you.

  Warning: Abraham had two sons. (4:21–31)

    Allegory:

      Hagar is Mount Sinai bearing children for slavery, corresponding to the present Jerusalem.

      Sarah is our mother who is free, the Jerusalem above.

        Citation: Isa. 54:1

    Applied:

      As Ishmael persecuted Isaac then, so it is now.

Citation: "Cast out the slave and her son." (Gen. 21:10–12)
Conclusion: So we are the children of the free woman.
Exhortation: (5:1—6:10)
Call to stand fast in Christ's freedom (5:1)
Warning against the enslavement of circumcision (5:2–12)
Warning against enslavement to the flesh (5:13–21)
Instruction in the fruits of the spirit (5:22–26)
Instructions in the "law of Christ" (6:1–10)
Epistolary Postscript: (6:11–18)
Including a final appeal: not circumcision, but the cross of Christ.

The argument is hot and hard, dependent on the force of logic (syl-logistic enthymemes), noninvented witnesses (kerygma as a fact, what the Galatians had experienced, Scripture as a written document), and au-thorities (Scripture as oracle, first apostles, assertions of Paul as a privileged authority), rather than upon analogies, maxims, multiple examples, and the soft development of themes. Apparently, the heat of social conflict and the debate about marks and codes of social identity forced such a consideration. The argument was focused on the relation between the Jewish Scriptures as the literal manifestation of Jewish culture and con-vention on the one hand and the kerygma of the early Christians on the other.

Paul's strategy was to manipulate both in the interest of his gospel. His treatment of the Torah as epic and oracle versus law, while audacious and self-serving if not contemptuous and dishonest, is nevertheless the more persuasive part of his plan. This is because Jews themselves were actively engaged in just such reflection about their epic scriptures and in debate about where to locate the charter for new times and eventualities. Jewish Christians may not have liked what they heard, but they would have understood the nature of the argument. The weakest part of Paul's argument lies in the attempt to reinterpret the kerygma by aligning "Christ" with the promise to Abraham.

The logic of the kerygma already supported the "justification" of Gentiles in the new social experiment, and Jesus' death as a saving event was already linked loosely to the God of Israel's history (Rom. 3:25–26). But to elaborate that logic in order to prove that non-Jews were the true Jews, and that keeping the law no longer justified before God, required an additional series of mind-boggling extrapolations. Paul had to argue that Christ was the sole "seed" of Abraham, and that Christians were the true children of Abraham by being "in Christ," and therefore children of God, and therefore infused with the spirit of life, and therefore sole recipients of the promised blessing to Abraham. He had to argue for all of this on the basis of Christ's death as a redemption from the law which was a curse upon those who tried to keep it as their claim to the inheritance of Abraham's blessing. The logic of the kerygma was originally worked out by Jewish Christians who wanted to "justify" the inclusion of Gentiles even though they were "sinners." Paul's elaboration was now quite different. It was addressed to both Gentile and Jewish Christians who apparently did not want to justify Gentiles as "sinners," but to make them ritually "righteous." In opposition to this, Paul upped the ante to the point of all or nothing. His argument about the gospel was worked out to support his deliberative appeal to "stand fast" in "freedom" (from the law), a freedom that probably had not been necessary before the issue arose. It is therefore difficult to assess the effect of Paul's letter to the Galatians. Gentile Christians who had not entertained the arguments for circumcision would not have needed Paul's exhortation. Gentile Christians who had considered circumcision may not have been persuaded by his argument. Paul himself, judging from the Corinthian correspondence and his Letter to the Romans, later found it helpful to drop the Abraham's seed-Christ argument and enlarge his epic frame of reference to make more room for the inclusion of Jews in the divine plan.

C. THE EPISTLE TO THE HEBREWS

10. Examples of Faith: Heb 11:1—12:3

The well-known chapter on faith consists largely of a series of examples. "Faith" indeed! The term *pistis* was the technical term for a rhetorical proof, based on connotations stemming from Greek juridical usage: "credence," "persuasion," "confidence." And the example *(paradeigma)* was the primary form of proof for constructing a rhetorical argument. Thus Hebrews 11 presents a series of examples *(paradeigmatas)* of confidence *(pistis)* as proofs *(pisteis)*. Such an overlay of form, content, and function was not unusual in Hellenistic educational compositions, but it does seem to be an extremely sophisticated form of reflection for early Christian mythmaking. This studied nuance, moreover, is hardly the sum of the rhetorical cleverness involved. The other major type of proof, forming a fundamental pair with the example, was "nonrhetorical evidence," which included such things as "witnesses," laws, documents, precedent judgments, and the like. If one notices that the examples of persuasion were taken from the Scriptures, that scriptural citation could serve as a witness in deliberative theses, and that the examples are said (and cited) to have been attested by God (the witness supreme) and to function as witnesses for the reader (12:1), then the strategy by which these figures were charged with rhetorical force is disclosed. Hebrews 11 is not a simple list of inadequate illustrations of the Christian notion of belief. These examples are evidence for the rhetorical process by which the Christian notion of faith came to be.

The series of examples forms the body of a rhetorical unit that must be carved out of the "continuous" style of discourse for which Hebrews is known. It is relatively easy to identify the unit, however, for the theme of *pistis* runs from 11:1 to 12:3, a period that makes sense on other grounds as well. There is an introduction, the series of examples broken thematically into two distinct sections, and the climactic portrayal of Jesus as the example par excellence followed by an exhortation. Persuasion is achieved by the scope of the series, a rather judicious classification of the scriptural accounts, a careful balance between emphases on the exemplars versus emphasis on the common virtue, and a ranking system that leaves Jesus in a class by himself without detracting from the honors due his precursors.

Ranking is achieved by following the sequence of the grand epic history of Israel with its implicit quest for a homeland. The reinterpretation of the homeland symbol allows the epic rehearsal to end not with Judea and the temple, but with Jesus, and the heavenly Jerusalem. One might conclude that the Israelite quest had been in vain. But the epic theme itself allowed these figures to be cast as illustrious precursors who were faithful *(pistos)* to a vision and its promise despite the fact that they did not see its fulfillment. The rhetorical topic is thus not one of contrast or opposition between Jesus and the epic of Israel, but of the good and the better, or the lesser/greater, a comparison that strikes one as constructive and assuaging.

The description of these exemplars is nevertheless calculated to cast them as precursors to Jesus. The themes of sacrifice, obedience, suffering, endurance unto death, and rescue are emphasized as the signs of *pistis*, which, of course, they are in the martyrological rationale that underlay the kerygmatic interpretation of Jesus' death. This means that yet another consideration can be discerned in this study of "faithfulness," for *pistos* (faithful) is the fundamental virtue of the martyr. That these faithful examples are said to have performed certain deeds, or suffered certain fates "by faith" is therefore noteworthy. By faith (*en* with the dative) can just as easily be translated "in confidence" (i.e., of the vision) or "in faithfulness" (i.e., to the promise). It need not be taken as a dative of agency or effectiveness. The point of the whole unit is to encourage the imitation of these examples of obedient endurance, not to practice the effective faith that can move mountains!

Only an overview outline will be given in order to establish the rhetorical unit. The reader who dares to have a closer look will know that the details also are chock-full of rhetorical terminology and craft.

An Encomium on Pistis

I. **Introduction** (Heb. 11:1–3)
   Definition:
   Pistis is confidence in matters of hope;
   the conviction of things not visible.
   "Genealogy":
   By it the elders received divine attestation.
   By it we know the world to have been established by the speaking of God.

II. The **Virtues** and Blessings of Faith
   A. Paradigms from the primeval history: (11:4–12)
   Abel offered sacrifice and was approved.
   Enoch pleased God and was translated.
   Noah saved his house and proved righteous.
   Abraham obeyed the call to sojourn.
   Sarah received power to conceive.
   B. Summary: (11:13-16)
   All of these died in confidence without receiving the promised homeland they were seeking.
   C. The patriarchs as paradigms: (11:17–28)
   Abraham passed the test by "offering up" Isaac and "receiving him back from the dead."
   Isaac invoked future blessings on his sons.
   Jacob, when dying, blessed each of the sons of Joseph.
   Joseph, at the end of his life, anticipated the exodus.
   Moses kept the Passover and led the exodus.

III. **The Deeds** and Achievements of Faith
   A. Exemplars of entrance to the land: (11:29–31)
   The people crossed over.
   Jericho fell down.
   Rahab did not perish.
   B. The judges and prophets: (11:32–34)
   There is not time enough to tell of Gideon, Barak, Samson, Jephthah, David, Samuel, and the prophets.
   They conquered kingdoms, enforced justice, received promises, stopped the mouths of lions, quenched fire, escaped the sword, won strength from weakness, became mighty in war, and put armies to flight.
   C. The women and martyrs: (11:35–38)
   Women received their dead by resurrection.

Some were tortured, refused release, that they might rise to
a better life.
Others suffered mocking and scourging, chains, imprisonment.
They were stoned, sawn in two, killed with the sword. They
went about in skins of sheep and goats, destitute, afflicted,
ill-treated, wandering over deserts and mountains, and in
dens and caves of the earth.
Of these the world was not worthy.
   D. Summary: (11:39–40)
All these, though well attested by their faith, did not receive
what was promised, since God had foreseen something bet-
ter for us, that apart from us they should not be made perfect.
IV. **Memorial** to the Paradigm par excellence: (12:1–3)
   A. Analogy: The race:
Since we are surrounded by so great a cloud of witnesses,
Let us also lay aside every weight,
And run the race with perseverance.
   B. Paradigm: Jesus.
Looking to Jesus, the pioneer and perfecter of our faith.
   He endured the cross,
   despised the shame,
   and is seated at the right hand of the throne of God.
   C. Exhortation:
Consider him, who endured such hostility,
so that you may not grow weary or fainthearted.

Hebrews 11 is a fine example of polished rhetorical composition. Its
attractiveness and persuasive power are due to an even distribution of
techniques executed with care. It makes use of stylistic, tropic, and im-
agistic refinements in a well-balanced format. It does not overplay the
extremely erudite manipulation of terminology, concepts, metaphors, and
allusions that can be found throughout. It thus encapsulates its argumentation in a soft tenor. The argument is also suave, won by judicious
selection of examples and their arrangement by topic and theme. Ultimately, to be sure, the persuasion rides on two enculturated authorities,
the Scriptures as Jewish epic and the Christian kerygma of the founding
event of Christ's death and resurrection. These are merged to form a story
of common quest for a better homeland, a story without kings, a quest
worth the sufferings and sacrifices endured in confidence. To be invited
to join such a crowd of witnesses may have been an effective exhortation.
Applied to the problems of duress, weariness, and apostasy in the Jewish-
Christian community addressed by the treatise, this encomium on confident faithfulness may have proven quite helpful.

11. An Exhortation to Accept Discipline: Heb 12:5–17

A marvelous elaboration on the theme of discipline is appended to the encomium on *pistis* by means of a reminder that the Christians addressed had not yet struggled to the point of shedding their blood (12:4). A citation from Proverbs (3:11–12) is set forth as the thesis, and the elaboration unfolds on the classroom model. Only the paradigm is missing from the standard list of components, but that can be explained by the position of this exhortation in the treatise. No illustrious example would be either necessary or appropriate following upon the examples given in the preceding encomium on faith(fulness). Thus the elaboration assumes that the proof by example (paradigm) has already been given, and offers instead a reflection on "endurance" as "discipline," a way of imagining how an ordinary Christian might see oneself among that cloud of witnesses to faith.

An Exhortation

Introduction: (Heb. 12:5)

> Have you forgotten the exhortation which addresses you as sons?
> "My son, do not regard lightly the discipline of the Lord,
> nor lose courage when you are punished by him.

Thesis: (12:5–6)

> For the Lord disciplines him whom he loves,
> And chastens every son whom he receives."

Paraphrase: (12:7a–b)

> It is for discipline that you have to endure.
> God is treating you as sons.

Argument:

Example: (12:7c)

> For what son is there whom his father does not discipline?

Opposite: (12:8)

> If you are left without discipline, which all experience, then you are illegitimate children and not sons.

Example: (12:9–10)

> We respect earthly fathers who discipline us.
> Shall we not much more be subject to the Father of spirits and live?
> For our earthly fathers disciplined us for a short time at their pleasure,

Reason: (12:10)

> But he disciplines us for our good, that we may share his holiness.

Maxim: (12:11)

> For the moment all discipline seems painful rather than pleasant;

Later it yields the peaceful fruit of righteousness to those who
have been trained by it.
Conclusion: (12:12–17)
Citation: (Paraphrase of Isa. 35:3) (12:12–13)
Therefore lift your drooping hands,
and strengthen your weak knees,
and make straight paths for your feet,
so that what is lame may not be put out of
joint but rather be healed.
Exhortation: (12:14)
Strive for peace with all men, and for holiness without which
no one will see the Lord.

Proverbial wisdom is used to offer instruction on divine discipline
(paideia). The author draws upon the conventional distinction in Hellenistic Jewish wisdom literature between punishment and chastisement,
as well as upon the traditional wisdom notion of two stages. The first stage
is one of discipline; the second is one of grace and blessing. The authorities
that are marshaled in this brief exhortation are impressive: Jewish wisdom,
prophetic appeal, Deuteronomic law, epic example, human example, Jewish-Christian ethic (holiness, morality, purity, righteousness), and Hellenistic popular philosophy. The Hellenistic component has been assim-
ilated to a Jewish-Christian discourse, but it is discernible in the use of
the pattern of elaboration, the educational pedagogy, and especially in
the maxim (v. 11). The maxim is a thinly veiled reworking of a stock saying,
frequently attributed to Isocrates, "The root of education *(paideia)* is
bitter, but its fruit is sweet." For the Greeks, the bitter root was the labor
required by the educational process; the sweet fruit was the virtue to be
achieved. The author of Hebrews used the term *paideia* in its Jewish
wisdom nuance of discipline, and preferred the "peaceful fruit of righteousness" as the object of the training *(gymnasma)*. The result is a fine
accommodation of Hellenistic Jewish educational wisdom in support of a
Christian ethical appeal.

D. THE GOSPELS AND ACTS

In the Gospels, Jesus materials and the Christ kerygma were merged
to form the narrative of the "ministry" and "passion" of Jesus-Christ. This
meant that the teachings of Jesus were given a new scenic setting complete
with plot and consequences. A discussion of the rhetoric of the Gospels
would therefore have to begin with a theory of narrative as communication,
move to the narrative logic of a teacher who was crucified, and explicate
the rhetorical force of teachings emanating from such a figure as Jesus

the Christ, as well as the persuasive features of the story itself as story. Classical rhetoric did not develop a theory of narrative, and modern narrative theory is just now exploring the question of the rhetoric of story. We have learned that setting, characterization, event, sequence, plot, and resolution all carry rhetorical effect, but this effect has been explained in terms of aesthetic theories of the imagination, not in terms of argumentation or persuasion. It is therefore premature to discuss the rhetoric of the Gospels as narrative compositions.

It is true that Aristotle's *ars poetica* included pungent observations about the meaning *(dianoia)* of characterization *(ethos)* and plot *(mythos)* at the point of narrative resolution, especially in terms of tragic plots. But "meaning" was described pathetically, not in terms of persuasion, and studies that move from Aristotle and the tragedies to the Gospels have therefore been pursued mainly at the level of literary criticism. It is also true that classical rhetoric addressed the question of narrative, but only as a description of the case to be argued. The narratio of a speech was the place to clarify the who, what, where, when, and why of a single action or event that had come under scrutiny. Only in the case of an encomium did the rhetors suggest an organization of data on the outline of a sequence from birth to death, but this outline was imagined solely as a topical convenience, not as a plot with "issue," development, and resolution. When approaching narrative literature for the purposes of rhetorical analysis, therefore, the rhetors looked only for small segments within larger works (such as histories or tragedies), and especially for scenes rich in description and speeches.

The ancient rhetorical understanding of narrative does bear upon the composition of the Gospels. One can see, for instance, that the piling up of scenic episodes in which Jesus addresses the situation receives some clarification. One can also see that the concern for description, though limited mainly to appropriate settings and audiences, corresponds to rhetorical requirements. It is also the case that the kinds of proof associated with the rhetorical narratio tend to predominate in the scenic narrative sections of the Gospels. These proofs, however, were technically of the noninvented kind. They consisted of witnesses, attestations, documentary evidence, and the like, all with the purpose of establishing the facts of the case. One might look at the role of the disciples, the miracles, and the prophetic citations from this point of view.

And yet, the Gospels are not prolegomena to a rhetorical speech. Neither is it adequate to limit their purpose to the establishment of the facts of the case. Their rhetoric bursts the bounds of mythological imagination, to say nothing of the normal rubrics for historical description. An assessment of their purpose has to begin with the observation that a high

Christology from the kerygmatic traditions (focused upon death and resurrection) was merged with a view of Jesus as a superior teacher and founder figure from the Jesus movements. Neither the purpose nor the imaginative-rhetorical persuasion of that merger has yet been adequately described. Nevertheless, some observations can be made about the difference it made for the content and rhetoric of the teachings when placed in the new narrative frame.

By framing the teachings of Jesus with the narrative plot of the appearance and crucifixion of God's Son, even sayings that were common, banal, and/or aphoristic in their pre-Gospel settings were given a different nuance. That is because the authority of the speaker, even if already enhanced as became a superior teacher of divine wisdom, was now linked to his role as crucified Savior and coming judge. The teachings, and especially the little speech clusters, polemical dialogues, and apocalyptic pronouncements, also became part of the plot. And the imperatival address to his followers now became the standard by which judgments of eternal consequence would fall. Thus the plot of the Gospels provided a new narratio, or scenic occasion, for hearing the teachings of Jesus and interpreting their significance.

It might also be mentioned that the rhetorical features inherent in the speech material did contribute to the narrative designs of the Gospels. Both genres (speech and extended narrative) shared certain objectives. Characterization (narrative) and the establishment of *ethos* (rhetoric) could complement each other. The speech occasion (rhetoric) could be used as an event (narrative) with significance for the plot. And the issues at stake in rhetorical debates could be used to establish the conflict in need of narrative resolution. The authors of the Gospels took advantage of each of these correlations.

The illustrations that follow, however, have been selected with a more limited purpose in mind. Speech material has been chosen on the basis of three criteria. (1) Each sayings unit has some features that are distinctive for the Gospel in which it occurs, consisting in most cases of sayings that occur only in that Gospel. (2) The unit reflects the author's design for the Gospel narrative as a whole. (3) The unit exhibits a rhetorical pattern of argumentation.

12. Discipleship Sayings in Mark: Mark 8:34—9:1

Scholars agree that these instructions in discipleship are Mark's composition, carefully placed at that point in his narrative where the predictions of the passion are given on the way to Jerusalem. There is some overlap of individual sayings with the Sayings Source (Q), but these sayings now occur in a unit of speech that clearly reflects the Markan plot.

A Thesis on Discipleship

Setting: Jesus called the crowd and his disciples to him for the instruction. (v. 34)

Thesis: If one wants to be a disciple, one must deny oneself, take up one's cross, and follow him. (v. 34)

   Reason: Whoever loses his life for the sake of Jesus and the gospel will save it. (v. 35)

Argument:

  The Opposite: Whoever seeks to save his life will lose it. (v. 35)

   Analogy: Gain in a transaction:

What profit is there to gain the whole world and lose one's life?

What can one give in return for his life? (vv. 36-37)

   Example: Whoever is ashamed of me and my words now in this world, of him the Son of man will be ashamed when he comes in the glory of his Father. (v. 38)

Pronouncement:

Truly I say to you, there are some standing here who will not taste death before they see the kingdom of God come with power. (9:1)

Proverbial wisdom about the priceless value of life has been (rather awkwardly) used in support of a mimetic martyrology that promises salvation. The theme of salvation is supported by projecting an apocalyptic future, the finality of which is underscored by the negative example (warning) and the positive pronouncement. Thus the instruction is a deliberative argument formulated in terms of the Gospel's plot. The plot combines a martyrological passion narrative with an apocalyptic resolution. That it serves as a paradigm for the instruction in discipleship is indicated, not only by the argument and its theme but also by the description of discipleship as a "following" of Jesus. The force of the argument derives ultimately from the astounding authority of the speaker, achieved by compounding the roles of founder teacher, crucified Christ, predictive prophet, and apocalyptic judge.

13. The Sermon on the Mount in Matthew: Matthew 5–7

Most of the material in Matthew's Sermon on the Mount comes from the Sayings Source (Q). Matthew's arrangement, however, is distinctively his own, as are a number of significant additions to the Q material, such as the section on the status of the law (5:17–20) and the emphasis on righteousness in the Beatitudes. Read in the light of Matthew's Gospel as a whole, the sermon is designed to support his depiction of Jesus as the inaugurator of a new ethic of righteousness.

This ethic was understood by Matthew to be a kind of law, superior to the Jewish law in some ways, but derived from it in others. He therefore had to present the teachings of Jesus as law in comparison and contrast with the Jewish law, and at the same time establish the authority of Jesus to have instigated such a novel revision. Matthew's Gospel was written to establish that authority. The issue of the two laws was worked out primarily in the sermon.

The details of the argumentation are too numerous and complex to explicate fully here, but an outline can be given that highlights the rhetorical pattern and design. The speech follows the deliberative outline, although two theses have to be addressed simultaneously. One is that Jesus' teaching fulfills the law. The other is that followers should therefore obey his words. Since the sermon is also the first statement of the content of Jesus' teachings, however, the argument does not unfold apart from the teachings, but uses them to make the argument. This accounts for the several lists of examples under each heading. By listing examples of the new law that Jesus introduced, the new laws could be introduced as examples, analogies, and exhortations in support of the thesis.

The Sermon on the Mount

Speech Setting:	Mountain, crowd, disciples, teaching (Matt. 5:1–2)
Exordium: (Complimentary address to ideal audience)	
	Blessings on the righteous who are meek, poor in spirit, and persecuted
	Theirs is the new age.
	They/you are the salt of the earth, the light of the world. (5:3–16)
Narratio: (Two theses set forth as deliberative argument) (5:17–20)	
First Thesis:	I came to fulfill the law;
Opposite:	Not to abolish the law.
Reason:	What is written is written until heaven and earth pass away.
Second Thesis:	(As an authoritative pronouncement) Unless your righteousness exceeds that of the scribes and Pharisees, you will never enter the kingdom.
Reason:	Whoever relaxes the least important commandment shall be least in the kingdom.
Opposite:	Whoever does the commandments shall be called great.
Argumentation:	
I. **Examples**:	(of fulfilling the law by exceeding the law)
A. Murder	(5:21–26)

82

Antithesis:	The law prescribes judgment for killing. I say, for anger.
Example:	Insults
Example:	Labeling as a fool
New law:	First be reconciled; then make offering.
Maxim:	Agree quickly with your adversary.
Moral:	If you don't, you will pay.
B. Adultery	(5:27–30)
Antithesis:	The law proscribes adultery. I say, lust.
Example:	Looking lustfully at a woman
New law:	Get rid of the offending member.
Example:	If your right eye offends . . .
Reason:	It is better . . .
Example:	If your right hand offends . . .
Reason:	It is better . . .
C. Divorce	(5:31–32)
Antithesis:	The law permits divorce.
New law:	I say, if you divorce, you make your wife an adulteress; if you marry a divorced woman, you commit adultery.
Exception:	On the ground of unchastity
D. Swearing	(5:33–37)
Anthithesis:	The law proscribes false swearing.
New law:	I say, do not swear at all.
Examples:	By heaven, by earth, by Jerusalem
Reason:	They are God's.
Example:	By your head
Reason:	You can't do anything to change it.
New law:	Let your yes be yes, and your no, no.
Reason:	Anything more is evil.
E. Retaliation	(5:38–42)
Antithesis:	The law prescribes an eye for an eye. I say, do not resist one who is evil.
Examples: (of the new law):	
	If one strikes you on the cheek, then turn the other also. If one takes your coat, let him have your tunic as well. If one forces you to go one mile, go with him two. Give to him who begs or borrows.
F. Love and hate	(5:43–48)
Antithesis:	The law says to love your neighbor and hate your enemy.

New law: I say, love your enemy . . .
Reason: So that you may be children of the Father.
Pos. Example: How the Father treats all
Analogies: Sun, rain, on both just and unjust
Neg. Example: Tax collectors; Gentiles
Analogy: Rewards
New law: You must be perfect, as your Father.
II. **Examples:** (of a more perfect piety):
Principle: Do not practice piety publicly. (6:1)
A. Alms   (6:2–4)
Neg. code: Do not make a show of giving alms.
Neg. Example: Hypocrites in synagogues and streets
Analogy: Sounding a trumpet in advance
Reason: They are rewarded by human praise.
Pos. code: Give alms secretly.
Analogy: Left hand not knowing what the right hand does.
Reason: God will reward you.
B. Prayer   (6:5–15)
Neg. code: Do not make a show of praying in public.
Neg. Example: Hypocrites in synagogues and street corners
Reason: They have their reward by being seen.
Pos. code: Pray in secret.
Example: Shut the door and pray before God.
Reason: God will see and reward.
Paradigm: The Lord's Prayer
Reason: If you forgive, you will be forgiven.
                If you don't, you won't be.
C. Fasting   (6:16–18)
Neg. code   Do not look dismal.
(Elaboration follows the above pattern.)
(**Argumentation** Pattern Continues: 6:19–24)
Analogies: (appropriate to the immediately preceding, but in support of the sermon as a whole):
                Treasure in heaven.
                The eye and the lamp.
Maxim: No one can serve two masters.
Exhortations: (prohibitive)
A. Do not be anxious. (6:25–34)
    (A full elaboration)
B. Do not judge. (7:1–5)
    (A condensed elaboration)
C. Do not broadcast your precious knowledge. (7:6)
    (Two analogies plus supporting reason)

Exhortations: (positive)
   A. Ask, and it will be given you. (7:7–12)
      (A full elaboration)
   B. Enter by the narrow gate. (7:13–14)
      (A condensed elaboration)
Warnings:
   A. Against false prophets. (7:15–20)
      Analogies: wolves, trees, and fruits
   B. Not everyone who says Lord, Lord shall enter. (7:21–23)
   C. Parable of the house on rock and sand. (7:24–27)
Narrative conclusion: (7:28–29)
   The crowds were astonished, for he taught them as one who had authority, not as their scribes.

The persuasive power of the Sermon on the Mount ultimately rests on the authority of Jesus as the founder of the new movement. This authority was enhanced, however, by subsuming the cultural tradition of the Jewish law. Matthew cleverly found a way to interpret the Q tradition as a new and superior law by arguing that it captured the ethics of the Jewish law at the level of intention and internalization. The force of the argument lies in the arrangement of the Q material as a deliberative speech and in the vivid imagery it provided in contrast to the caricature of the scribes and Pharisees. The comparison is such that the moralism of the new law is seen to be superior. The contrast between public and divine approval also allows for a legal justification of the natural theology of Q.

14. The Preaching of John the Baptist: Luke 3:1–18

The Lukan version of the preaching of John is highly elaborate in comparison to Q, Mark, and Matthew. Luke provides encomiastic touches in line with his earlier narratives of the miraculous birth of John, the angel's poetic prediction that John would fulfill Elijah's role, and his father Zechariah's hymn of praise. When Luke comes to the preaching of John, he mentions that the word of the Lord came to John in the wilderness, and he extends the citation from Isaiah about the "voice of one crying in the wilderness" to include the saying that "all flesh shall see the salvation of God" (Luke 3:6). This mention of salvation stands in tension with John's mention of the wrath to come (v. 7), but it agrees with Luke's conclusion that John's preaching was "good news" (v. 18) and thus brackets the otherwise mainly judgmental predictions. The exception to this theme of judgment is Luke's own addition to the tradition (vv. 10–14) where John gives explicit instructions about what one should do in order to "bear fruits worthy of repentance." Luke calls the sermon an exhortation (v. 18), a form of deliberative rhetoric.

John's Preaching

Narrative:	John is preaching in the wilderness a baptism of repentance for the forgiveness of sins. (vv. 2–3)
Citation:	The prophet Isaiah (vv. 4–6)
Chreia:	When the crowds came out to be baptized, he said, "You brood of vipers! Who warned you to flee from the wrath to come?" (v. 7)
Thesis:	One should bear fruits worthy of repentance. (v. 8a)

Argumentation:

I. Refutation of anticipated rebuttal: Do not start to say that Abraham is your father. (v. 8b)

Reason:	Being children of Abraham is not enough. (v. 8b)
Contrary:	God can raise up children from the stones. (v. 8c)
Analogy:	Every tree that does not bear good fruit is cut down and burned. (v. 9)

II. Exhortation: What specifically one should do (vv. 10–14)

Example:	The crowds: Let them share. (v. 11)
Example:	Tax collectors: Don't cheat. (vv. 12–13)
Example:	Soldiers: No violence (v. 14)

Conclusion:

Warning:	A mightier one is coming. (vv. 15–16)
Analogy:	Separating the chaff from the grain (v. 17)
Exhortation:	Good news with exhortation (v. 18)

Luke's version of John's sermon is not particularly convincing because the resulting mixture of tradition with new interpretation is not successful. The tradition from Q and Mark was decidedly an announcement of wrath and judgment. It was argued by means of the prophetic witness and two analogies of separation and destruction (John's warning about what happens to bad trees, and the description of Jesus' "baptism" as a harvest). Luke tried to recast the purpose of John's preaching as "good news" by suggesting that repentance paved the way for the time of salvation. He did so by expanding the prophetic citation, by giving three examples of bearing good fruit, and by asserting that the message was an exhortation to repentance. Supposing that John's sermon on the coming judgment was familiar to Luke's audience (had been accepted as persuasive in the context of the gospel narrative), and that there was no longer need for such an overt polemic against Jewish detractors, Luke's additions may have been enough to shift the point of the preaching from wrath to salvation. Note that the examples suggest a largely Gentile milieu. Note also that, though the Q-Mark persuasion rests ultimately on the appeal to a double witness (the prophetic witness to John, and John's witness to Jesus), Luke's version finally appeals to the appearance of John and Jesus as historically significant, and to the content of the exhortation itself as acceptable ethic.

15. The Witnesses to Jesus in John: John 5:30–47

Following upon the story of the healing of the lame man at the pool of Bethzatha, John announces the plot of the Jews to kill Jesus because he "called God his Father, making himself equal with God" (5:18). This leads into a monologue on the theme of the Son's ability to make "judgments." The point is that he does not do so on his own, but only because he knows and obeys the Father's will. Then the issue of evidence for such a claim is raised, and a typically Johannine meditation is given on the "witnesses" to Jesus' special status. The section is modeled on that portion of a judicial speech in which the evidence is evaluated. The reader needs to keep in mind that the theme of making judgments in John is loaded with dialectical connotation.

The Second Witness

Exordium:	(Narrativized: Jesus at Bethzatha)
Narratio:	(Jesus is from the Father; 5:19–30)
Issue:	(Assumed: a second witness needed)
The Partition of the Evidence. (5:31)	
Argument:	

1. The witness of John the Baptist. (5:33–35)

Type:	A human eyewitness.
Validity:	He bore witness to the truth.
Invalidation:	I do not accept human testimony.

2. The miracles I perform. (5:36)

Type:	Manifest deeds.
Validity:	They bear witness that the Father has sent me.

3. The Father who sent me. (5:37–38)

Type:	Agency.
Validity:	He himself has borne witness to me.
Invalidation:	You have never heard his voice or seen his form.
Reason:	You do not have his word abiding in you.
Reason:	You do not believe the one he sent.

4. The Scriptures: (5:39–44)

Type:	Documentary.
Validity:	They bear witness to me.
Invalidation:	You search the Scriptures thinking to have life; yet you refuse to accept me.
Reason:	You do not have the love of God in you.

Example:	You will receive one who comes in his own name;
	yet you will not receive me though I came in the Father's name.
Example:	You receive glory from one another; and do not seek the glory that comes from God.
Conclusion:	How can you believe?

Conclusion (both to 4 and to the entire chapter): (5:45–46)

Statement:	It is not I who accuse you.
Opposite:	It is Moses who accuses you.
Reason:	Moses wrote about me;
	yet you do not believe me.
	Therefore, you do not believe Moses.
	If you don't believe Moses' words,
	How will you believe my words?
Assumed accusation:	The "judgments" you make about me will determine the "judgments" made about you.

Syllogistic reasoning in John is frequently masked by the ellision or displacement of one of its premises, or by proposing a deductive argument on the basis of an inductive conclusion. The circular reasoning is carried by the spiral effect of the discourse and the layered connotations of its symbols. Reduced to the normal rules of reasoning, Johannine argumentation is patently illogical. If compared with the normal rules of rhetoric, it is not persuasive. When compared with normal occasions of communication, it is marked by inauthenticity. Nevertheless, those within the community, accustomed to the imaginative mythology of Jesus as the divine Logos, may have found Jesus' speech intriguing. Its challenge was essentially semantic and played on the dialectic between two connotations of the term logos—speech as logical and narrative as completed event. Both connotations were merged in the figure of Jesus as the Logos and their logics were inverted in the interest of emphasizing the astounding authority Jesus had for them.

16. Peter's Pentecost Sermon: Acts 2:1–42

Luke's program turned the Gospel narrative into a chapter of epic history. In Acts the apostles are preachers of the gospel-in-miniature which, in turn, gained its significance as the goal toward which the history of Israel had unfolded. The events of significance in all three phases of the epic history (the time of Israel, Jesus, and the church) were, according to Luke, speech occasions. The speech occasion of importance was, moreover, prophetic, combining a call to repentance with a promise of salvation.

The three phases were joined together by interlocking these speech occasions, so that the speech to Israel predicted the Christ, Christ predicted the time of salvation or the church, and the apostles continued to preach (promise) salvation by rehearsing the history of prophetic activity. In each period, the message was accepted by some, rejected by others.

In retrospect, the fate of the previous preachers became part of the message. Their personal fate was taken as an attestation of the truth of their message, as was its rejection by those to whom it was delivered and its fulfillment in the next chapters of the Christian epic. This meant that, for Luke, preaching was narrative rehearsal as well as a performance of the prophetic activity of calling for repentance and promising salvation. Thus the sermons in Acts are largely (a) narrative correlations of the time of Jesus with predictive promises from the time of Israel, and (b) demonstrations that the present preaching occasion follows upon the pattern of prophetic activity.

Demonstration for Luke is therefore largely a matter of stacking up privileged examples from each era and citing "witnesses" that attest to their interlocking. Interlocking is achieved in the first place by creating correspondences among the paradigmatic events. Syncrisis is thus a favorite technique, as is exegetical ingenuity in the signification of scriptural terms and themes that can be taken to refer beyond themselves to the subsequent events of fulfillment. The conceptual principle of continuity is the Spirit of God, which Luke uses to relate prophetic speech to prophetic destiny, as well as episodes from era to era. In the times of Jesus and the apostles, miracles can also be used as a major witness to the presence of the Spirit of God and of the validity of prophetic activity. Thus the argumentation in Acts is truncated from a rhetorical point of view. That is because it is primarily concerned with a narratio that highlights the nontechnical type of proof, making use of syllogistic reasoning to establish connections among the stacked-up examples. The syllogistic reasoning is, moreover, weak, frequently not even expressed. And there is hardly any supporting argumentation that elaborates the reasons for prophetic assertions. The sermons, nonetheless, are cast as exhortations; they follow the form of deliberative speech and are given narrative settings that assert their effectiveness as persuasive speeches. Thus, any outline of a sermon in Acts must include the narrative of its setting, because the response of the audience is intended by Luke to be taken as an on-the-spot proof of the truth preached by the apostles.

Peter's Sermon
Narrative Setting: (Acts 2:1–13)
  Pentecost as the time and place

Three interlocking miracles of speech reported:
    Filled with the Spirit
    Speaking in all languages
    Content of the speaking: the mighty works of God
Audience: Jews from every nation gathered in Jerusalem
Issues raised:
    a) What must this mean?
    b) Are they drunk?
Peter's Sermon:

Exordium:	Men of Judea . . . (v. 14)
Narratio:	(of the occasion) (vv. 15–21)
Refutation:	These are not drunk.
Reason:	It is 9:00 A.M.
Assertion:	It is the Spirit of God.
Citation:	Joel 2:28–32:
	"I will pour out my spirit. . . .
	Whoever calls on the name of the Lord shall be saved."

(Implied issues: Proof that it is the Spirit, that it has to do with salvation, that one should therefore call on the name of the "Lord.")

Partition of the Issues for **Proof:**

A. Proposition: God raised Jesus up.

Citation:	Psalm of David 16:8–11.
	(Saw/Lord/Right hand/did not abandon to Hades)
Refutation:	It is not about David.
Reason:	David died and was not raised.
Witness:	His tomb.
Assertion:	It was a prophecy about Christ.
Witness:	God's oath to David
Witness:	God's promise to David (of a royal descendant)
Conclusion:	"Not abandoned to Hades" means Christ's resurrection.
Witness:	We are his witnesses.
B. Proposition:	Resurrection means exalted "to the right hand." There Jesus received the "promise" of the Spirit and "poured it out" on us.

Proof implied from previous citations:

	David saw him up there. (Psalm 16)
	God's promise to David was the Spirit prophesied in Joel.
Witness:	What you (audience) see and hear
Citation:	David's Psalm 110:1
	(The Lord said to my Lord . . .)

Epilogue: God made Jesus both Lord and Christ . . .
                       whom you crucified.

Narrative Setting:

Cut to the heart, "What shall we do?"

Peter's Response:

Exhortation: Repent and be baptized in the name of Jesus
                       Christ for the forgiveness of sins.

Promise: You will receive the gift of the Holy Spirit.

Reason: The promise is to all . . . "everyone whom the
                       Lord our God calls to him." (An invisible citation
                       from Joel 2:32)

Narrative conclusion:

And Peter testified with many other words and exhorted them.

Peter's Warning: Save yourselves from this generation.

Those who received the word were baptized.

The argument here is obviously pitched for the readers of Acts. They are invited to imagine the occasion for the first Christian sermon, one that did not address them personally, but rather the Jews of all nations. Jews who had not already become Christians would not have been engaged by this sermon, much less convinced. Reasons why Jews would have wanted to repent and be forgiven are not evident. The sermon is conceived to support the narrator's description of Pentecost as the birth of the church, and the proofs it contains all support that end. Thus the scriptural witnesses are interwoven with the occasional witnesses, and the explication of the gospel is focused on making the link between resurrection and the pouring out of the Spirit. The entire Lukan theology of the epic plan of salvation must be assumed just to make minimal sense of the many connections among the witnesses that are required.

At the surface level of the text, rhetorical attention is paid only to one of the three scriptural citations, David's Psalm 16. The Joel citation is not elaborated, but set forth as the prediction that explains Pentecost. Luke knew, however, that the Joel citation itself was in need of explication, for the point is later made about the promise to David being the Spirit Jesus received from God when exalted. The point about Jesus as David's Lord was needed in order to apply the Joel saying about "calling on the name of the Lord" to the occasion of being baptized "in the name of Jesus Christ" whom "God made Lord." These points also are made simply by assertion; they are not argued. The only serious attempt at argumentation, therefore, is to establish the connection between Ps. 16:8–11 and the resurrection of Jesus. It is weak, consisting mainly of the negative point that David could not have been talking about himself. The positive witnesses connected with David (God's oath and promise to him) are not derived from the Psalm text, explained as connectors, embellished as concepts, or supported as arguments. This is a speech that follows the form of rhetorical persuasion, but gains its force only from the dramatic aspects of its narration.

Conclusion:

The Promise of Rhetorical Criticism

Rhetorical criticism should take its place as a discipline among the many other approaches to early Christian literature that define the work of New Testament scholarship. Rhetorical criticism should find it possible to complement the work of other criticisms and contribute to their learning. This is especially the case with its clearly defined and constructive liaisons with literary criticism and emerging methods for the analysis of social formations and histories. Its promise is that a rhetorical perspective on language and literature may make it possible to treat New Testament texts both as literary compositions and documents of early Christian social history at one and the same time. If so, rhetorical criticism would provide a bridge joining scholars trained in literary criticism and those trained in the social sciences. At the present time there is a noticeable gap between the ways each subdiscipline treats its textual data.

Rhetorical criticism may do more than build a bridge across that gap in scholarly interests and methods, however. That is because a rhetorical perspective on a piece of literature can render its own account of the social occasion for that literature. Rhetoric is capable of describing an exchange of words and ideas as a strategy by which an author seeks to influence his or her readers. Rhetoric therefore has the capacity of joining forces with other theoretical disciplines that seek to describe the dynamics of social intercourse and formation. Disciplines focused on a social anthropology of religion and culture are now in the process of defining the space between a society's theory and its practice (or symbol system and social enterprise), and the importance of that space is being emphasized as the arena within which all human activity is acknowledged, negotiated, reflected upon, and invested with social and personal significance. Rhetoric therefore opens up a perspective on the gap between what people say they believe and how they actually live. And since talking is the major gap activity of any human society, rhetorical criticism has a front-row seat for viewing this spectacular performance.

If the literature of the New Testament manifests the marks of rhetorical composition, this means that the texts in hand have been transfigured before our scholarly eyes. Suddenly the texts have turned into the data needed to describe a developing discourse, a discourse that may put us in touch with early Christianity as no other approach possibly can. Historical interest in the origins of early Christian movements was not one of the reasons for the inclusion of this literature in the canon, of course, so that these particular texts represent only the winners selected from what must have been a vigorously experimental period. Nevertheless, a rhetorical approach to the literature of the New Testament should give us some access to the social and ideological dynamics of the first-century movements and help us determine more precisely what exactly the new persuasion was.

Rhetoric cautions against taking the literature of the New Testament either at its face value or as a coded language for hidden theological truths whether timeless or recently revealed. Instead, rhetorical criticism explores the human issues at stake in early Christian social formation and its discourse. It seeks to render some account of the social issues that lay behind the rhetorical issues that surface in the literature of discourse. And it hopes to find some way to assess the quality of life reflected in the rhetoric, a quality that will be measured by the nature of that rhetoric itself. Since rhetoric has to do with the way in which we talk to and about one another, the unit of measurement for the scale is given. The quality of the exchange of ideas at the level of discourse will be used to measure the quality of human relations and exchanges throughout the arena of social intercourse.

A. THE DESCRIPTION OF A DISCOURSE

Early Christianity was a new social formation seeking to define itself within and over against both Jewish and Greek cultural traditions. To argue for a novel ethos meant that conventional views and patterns of persuasion had to be handled with care. If used as "proofs," even stock images, analogies, and examples from Greek or Jewish tradition would make their point by assuming the validity of their conventional cultures. What were early Christians to do?

What early Christians did was what any society involved in cultural change has to do: manipulate the stock images, conventional values, and standard rhetorical patterns of persuasion in the interest of their own social experiment and seek its grounding in some new system of recently anchored symbols. In order to catch early Christians at their craft, however, comparison with the standard practices and views is required. A number of differences between early Christian rhetoric and that of the cultures of context have already been mentioned, and these may now be summarized.

One distinguishing mark of early Christian discourse is a large incidence of figurative language. Metaphors, similes, analogies, and parables abound. Apparently, analogical discourse was less beholden to prevailing cultural traditions and could therefore be pressed into Christian service more easily than other forms of proof. One also notes that many of the analogies are intentionally odd, striking, or inversionary when compared to the way in which people usually behaved in the traditional social orders or the way things were thought to happen in the natural order. The impression in general is that early Christians were actively engaged in highly imaginative activity. One might extrapolate from this that Christian gatherings may have been lively occasions, and that part of the attraction may have been the intellectual stimulation occasioned by the social experimentation.

Another feature of early Christian discourse is the relative lack of historical examples from early Christian, Greek, or Jewish traditions. This can easily be explained by noting that early Christianity had not yet produced typical or illustrious examples, and that Greek and Jewish exemplars were inappropriate for the novel ethos. Greek heroes simply do not appear at all. The examples that were taken from Jewish epic tradition tended, moreover, to be used in contrast to usual Jewish interpretation. When positive examples were needed, early Christians struggled in the crosscurrents of two cultures that strongly disagreed about virtues, the manner of their achievement, and the value of their paradigmatic exemplification. Christians eventually settled on a singular and impossible exemplar (the Christ), and cast all other apostolic heroes in its image or shadow. But at first, in spite of the derring-do that must have accompanied early Christian leadership, early Christian rhetoric had no store of concrete human examples. Instead, an extremely vigorous Christian imagination created the ad hoc exemplum. Think of the options and imagine the impossible: "Seek the reign of God and all else will be added to you," "Sell your possessions and follow Jesus," "If your right hand offends, cut it off," "Whoever wants to follow me, let him take up his cross," "The reign of God is like a man . . . , a woman . . . , a farmer . . . , an estate owner . . . , a child (none of whose stories quite fit the way in which the world usually works). Given the fundamental importance of the paradigm for persuasion in classical rhetoric, the absence of the paradigmatic example in early Christian argumentation is a very significant datum. By filling in the vacant space with images of the impossible, early Christians may have been in danger of cultivating fantasies in place of this-worldly pieties and performances.

A third characteristic of early Christian speech is a high polemical quotient, bifocal address (to two audiences at once), and the prevalence of argument by negative contrast throughout entire argumentations. This reflects the process of social self-definition by means of comparison and contrast with the surrounding cultures of difference. It also identifies a problem that could easily get out of hand. The cultivation of a highly polemical stance and discourse can eventually come home to shape the mentality of a social formation. If a polemic gets locked into the logic of a group's fundamental persuasions, a pattern of thinking and perception can result that grows comfortable with an imagined message to outsiders that is essentially inauthentic as workable, social discourse. The pronouncement stories are a clear example of the cultivation of an inauthentic discourse. In them, the semblance of debate with those who disagree is elaborated over and over again. But the terms of the debate are always unfair and fictitious, weighted in advance in favor of the Christian's champion who must win in every round. In these stories the outsider, usually the Pharisees, becomes a straw man. If winning an argument against a straw man were to become a favorite imagination, models for conversation with those of different persuasions would be woefully inadequate, and in-house Christian discourse also would be in danger of falling into self-deceptions.

A fourth singularity is the issue of authority that overwhelms the reader of this discourse. Not only are the leaders of the various early Christian communities constantly in battle for the right to speak with authority, the practice of appealing to external authorities (Jesus, the Holy Spirit, or God) as guarantors for given propositions is also pervasive and strong throughout the literature. This is unusual in comparison with the tradition of Greek rhetoric, where persuasion was grounded in cultural convention without appeal to special authorization.

At first one might understand the quest for authorization as required by a new and experimental phase of social formation. But should the rhetoric of assertion, pronouncement, and "speaking with authority" become a habit, social structures could be created that cancel out the courage of critique that gave rise to the discourse in the beginning.

Thus it is that the distinguishing features of early Christian rhetoric become clues to the style and nature of a discourse-in-the-making. It is, of course, premature to project a reconstruction of that history. In tracing a few stages of particular traditions, we see that the movements were not monolinear. To make matters more complicated, the many early Jesus and Christ groups coming into view were not simply variations on a single social or ideological theme. Much more work needs to be done on the distinctive rhetorics of particular movements at specific junctures of their social histories. However, something can already be said about the process of social formation in general.

B. THE ANALYSIS OF A SOCIAL FORMATION

The issues under debate in units of argumentation describe and point to a set of problems encountered in the process of social formation. The profile is not at all mysterious. The normal requirements for self-definition all surface for adjudication: codes, social self-designations, leadership roles, boundary markers, distinguishing attitudes, practices and views, rituals, myths, and rites of entry and exclusion. In many cases it is possible to coordinate proposals for the solution of these problems with positions that were taken with regard to standard practices of the cultures of context. The various treatments of Greek and Jewish cultural vehicles are important indices to early Christian social formations and their necessary rationalizations. One example would be the variety of ways in which the Jewish Scriptures were taken, read, reinterpreted, and domesticated in each of the early Christian movements. Comparing the way in which the Scriptures were treated in the examples provided for Hebrews (see Part III, Section 10), Galatians (see Part III, Section 9), and Matthew's Sermon on the Mount (see Part III, Section 13), for instance, one is confronted with evidence for what must have been a vigorous labor in sorting through the Jewish Scriptures as an exercise in cultural positioning. Real social issues lurking in the background are not too difficult to discern, even though they differ from text to text and do not find a commonly recommended solution. Ultimately, however, neither the domestication of the Jewish Scriptures, nor the obligation to Hellenistic modes of thinking, or any other index to the ways in which early Christians carved out an accommodation to their cultures of context, cannot satisfy the social historian looking for the source of the new attraction. The proofs and persuasions set forth in our texts have to be seen as second-level inventions. They lack the power to have generated the convictions required by novel social experiments. Something else carried the day, and the imperfection of the rhetoric is a witness to it. By means of the analysis of this rhetoric, squiggles and all, what that something else may have been might come into view. One can already sense that it had something to do with the attraction of the social formation itself.

C. THE IDENTIFICATION OF AN EMERGING MYTHOS

The analyses have shown that early Christians struggled constantly with the question of authority. A first-level explanation is easy to formulate. The social critique basic to the impulse that lay at the foundation of the new movements rendered traditional authorities questionable. Experimentation on all fronts of social formation must have been encouraged at first, rather than prescribed behavior and appeals to precedence. Leadership soon had to become an issue, however, and the rhetoric reveals the heat of battles for the right to say what Christians should do. These battles mark much of the Pauline correspondence and thus appear at a relatively early but secondary stage of social formation and history.

We should note that, whereas Paul had to argue for his authority as an apostle, he never argued for the authority of the kerygma. In the Jesus traditions, moreover, the validity of what Jesus said might be in need of elaboration (e.g., supporting arguments for "loving one's enemy"), but his status as a teacher with authority to speak at all was apparently not in need of demonstration. A quick review of the examples in Part III above will show that in all cases the ultimate basis of the argumentation derives either (1) from Jesus as a teacher with authority, or (2) from the Christ kerygma. These agreements about Jesus as the founder teacher and about the Christ as the founder martyr can be called the core convictions of the new movements. Rhetorical criticism establishes the special status of these core convictions in all patterns of argumentation and persuasion. Were one so disposed, this evidence for the fundamental importance of these two convictions could be taken as an invitation to further reflection upon the particular values that emerged in the new religion. Closely related to these core convictions, at any rate, are such notions as special revelation, divine presence, transformation, justification, and mission.

There are ways to explain both of these agreements about where to locate ultimate authority, for each core conviction corresponds to a pattern of authorization current in the surrounding cultures, and both can be understood on the model of mythmaking in the interest of conceptualizing the new movements, a common human activity. The process by which each core conviction must have been first imagined, discussed, and elaborated can also be reconstructed. In the case of the Christ kerygma, for instance, arguments can be discerned in Rom. 3:25–26, 1 Cor. 15:3–5, and elsewhere, that certainly had to have been debated during the period of invention. In both cases, the fundamental logic is impeccable for the type of social formation it had to justify. And yet at the stage of social history and discourse represented by the New Testament texts, neither the unique authority of Jesus nor the originary significance of the kerygma were any longer in need of explication. In fact, the rhetoric reveals a certain unwillingness ever to let such questions arise again. It is this sense of the nonnegotiable that gives the rhetoric of the New Testament its peculiarly sharp edge.

Eventually, both locations of authority coalesced in the writing of the Gospels, and the myth of Christian origins took its place in conscious competition with the epics and myths of the cultures of context. Now Christianity had its own cluster of authoritative conventions and could venture forth as a self-sustaining culture in the midst of other traditions. At this late stage of textual tradition all of the smaller rhetorical units in the prior written traditions were subsumed by the narrative that combined the two core convictions in a single-level authorization. Everything in our texts—propositions, supporting arguments, analogies, oracles, laws, pronouncements, parables, stories, citations, asides and apostolic infelicities—could then be read off the top with the aura of inaugural address attached. This mode of reading the Bible became customary for the long history of the Christian churches and continues to prevail in living Christianity in the twentieth century. Rhetorical criticism joins with modern biblical scholarship in asking readers to have another look.

As do other critical approaches to the New Testament, rhetorical criticism seeks to gain perspective on a text by arresting the process of social and literary history at a given juncture. Each of the units of argumentation given as examples in Part III represents some specific moment in that early history. We must emphasize that those moments were way stations in the long process that eventually produced the New Testament. That the literary residue of each of those moments is now embedded in the New Testament is partly accidental, partly due to the judgments of diverse tradents who thought this or that piece of literature worthy of retention and partly a result of certain traditions winning out over others. These scholarly determinations of many specific rhetorical situations are not relevant to the reading of the New Testament as traditionally practiced by the church. In order for the New Testament to function as a charter document for the church, its final construction upon the first chapters of that history had to be accepted and all of the diverse moments and plural movements erased, even those that accidently contributed snippits of literary material to that final construction. That means that the rhetorics of occasional moments in the past became, by virtue of their retention and inclusion in the writings destined to become the New Testament, paradigmatic discourse, mythic models of the kind of speech that is now imagined to have generated Christianity (with Jesus) and to have characterized the originary chapters of the history of the church (with Paul).

Rhetorical criticism exposes the layered texture of the New Testament and thus the history of argumentation it unintentionally preserves. In doing so, a number of odd features pop up that result from the particular circumstances of the developmental history accidently retained in a unit of argumentation. The most interesting and serious oddity is the use of inductive forms and patterns of argumentation at a time when the authority to make theological pronouncements on any and every matter was already firmly in place (as, for instance, in Part III, Section 2). This could only have taken place during a period of transition in which the pattern of argumentation was still imagined in terms of debate even though the mode of argumentation had shifted drastically to pronouncement and threat. This circumstance is characteristic for the later layers of Q and for all of the pronouncement stories in the Gospels where Jesus' "debates" with the scribes and Pharisees are patently inauthentic exchanges. They are inauthentic as reports, for their logic does not follow the way in which the issues at stake must actually have arisen and been discussed before coming to resolution. And they are inauthentic as debates because there is no common ground to adjudicate. Jesus wins precisely because of his authority to make pronouncements with which his opponents would not have agreed. The danger is that, taken up into the Christian myth of origins, these residues of an understandable but unfortunate rhetorical history may be read as originary and taken as paradigmatic for Christian discourse. We can see what a disaster it would be if they were to become paradigmatic for Christian pronouncements aimed at those outside the borders. Rhetorical analysis helps to uncover the quality of a given exchange. It strikes to the core of these reported exchanges and exposes them as inauthentic discourse.

D. THE CHALLENGE TO A BIBLICAL HERMENEUTIC

The history of New Testament scholarship can be charted in two broadly defined courses. One is the critical investigation of the history and literature of early Christianity. The other is the periodic investigation of a relevant hermeneutic, usually one that is considered new. Historical scholarship is pursued in the interest of better understanding how Christianity came to be, and it brackets the question of the relevance of the New Testament for Christian faith and life. The hermeneutical quest is pursued in the knowledge that the New Testament functions as the charter document for the Christian religion, and in the interest of relating the results of scholarship to contemporary Christian concerns.

The history of hermeneutics is dotted with various theories of interpretation that allow the reader to move from the text (or times) as reconstructed by scholars to the world of human experience as known in modern times. In a sense, each period of scholarship and each criticism has grown out of contemporary ways of viewing and investigating the world, so that each "new" hermeneutic has been able to harvest the results of a period of biblical scholarship and bring its findings back to bear upon contemporary issues of Christian concern. A hermeneutic has nevertheless always been an extra, special endeavor, frequently born under its own banner, as, for instance, "demythologization," "existential interpretation," "aesthetic object criticism," and "parable theory" have functioned in the twentieth century. Each of these functioned as a hermeneutic that was anchored in a specifically scholarly discipline in touch with the thinking of its time.

Rhetorical criticism is no exception to this rule of the sociology of scholarship, for the scholarly interest in rhetoric can hardly be understood apart from its contemporary currency in a time of troubled discourse. Interest in rhetorical studies of any historical literature has its primary social context in the fact that the modern world also has become the object of rhetorical investigation and cultural critique. How we talk to each other across cultures, traditions, and ideological orientations makes all the difference in the world. To be about the task of exploring the rhetorics involved makes a great deal of sense in our time.

Rhetorical criticism of the New Testament does not depart from the long history of New Testament scholarship and its series of hermeneutics at the point of liaison with a modern academic sensibility and discipline. The difference lies at the point of the object and purpose of investigation. Traditionally, a hermeneutic has always been imagined on the model of a message that runs from the New Testament as speaker to the modern Christian as private listener. Philosophical and theological concerns have guided the investigation of the substance of the Christian message in the New Testament, the forms of its articulation there, and the hermeneutical question of how that message might again be "heard" in modern dress. The hermeneutical enterprise has been grounded in a romantic and individualistic anthropology in quest of a communication from God. Rhetorical criticism, on the other hand, prefers a social anthropology in order to describe adequately what we have been calling a discourse. This social perspective threatens to derail the history of philosophical and theological hermeneutics, because rhetorical criticism describes the equation of communication differently.

Rhetorical criticism takes the historical moment of a human exchange seriously in order to assess the quality of an encounter and the merits of an argumentation. It takes the social circumstances seriously in order to view the exchange from the perspective of each participant. Rhetorical criticism of the New Testament asks the modern reader to join the biblical critic in the work of judging the effectiveness of a human performance at a particular moment in early Christian history. It is not clear that these judgments will or should support traditional Christian views about the message of the New Testament and its relevance for instruction, faith, and piety.

Rhetorical criticism may therefore be the strongest challenge yet to the notion that critical scholarship and biblical hermeneutics should and will always come out together in support of some traditional definition of the Christian faith. In her presidential address in 1987, "The Ethics of Interpretation: Decentering Biblical Scholarship," Elizabeth Schüssler Fiorenza invited the Society of Biblical Literature to consider just such a reorientation of scholarly imagination. Rhetorical criticism, she said, would be the way to complement her call for decentering biblical scholarship and for listening to the many voices struggling to find a hermeneutic then and now. She stopped short of suggesting that rhetorical criticism might affect the way Christians have viewed the authority of the New Testament. But she was clear about the ethical issue of interpretation created by the social-historical circumstances of the twentieth century.

Our time demands a thorough investigation of the human capacity for dialogue and negotiation. It is not clear that the rhetoric of early Christians encountered in the New Testament will be a helpful model. The New Testament contains much early material that, if isolated and studied in social-historical context, arrests early Christian history at painful junctures of emergent self-definition where the rhetorics were harsh, divisive, and based upon non-negotiable claims to authority. Thus this rhetoric hardly matches either the full range of values most Christians ascribe to their religious heritage, or the challenge of our time for modes of conversation that can appreciate difference and bridge cultural barriers constructively. The hermeneutical value of a rhetorical criticism of the New Testament may therefore lie not in supplying models of discourse for twentieth-century Christians but in its challenge to the very notion of biblical hermeneutics as an essential grounding and guide for Christian faith and practice. If so, the new rhetorical criticism of early Christianity would be a scholarly event of historic proportions.

WORKS CITED

A. ANCIENT RHETORICAL TEXTS

Anaximenes. *Rhetorica ad Alexandrum*. Trans. H. Rackham. Loeb Classical Library (See Aristotle, vol. 16). Cambridge: Harvard University Press, 1937.

Aristotle. *The "Art" of Rhetoric (Ars Rhetorica)*. Trans. J. H. Freese. Loeb Classical Library. Cambridge: Harvard University Press, 1926.

Baldwin, C. S. *Medieval Rhetoric and Poetic*. New York: MacMillan, 1928. (Hermogenes' *Progymnasmata* in English on 23–38.)

Butts, James R. "The Progymnasmata of Theon. A New Text with Translation and Commentary." Ph.D. diss., Claremont Graduate School, 1986.

Cicero. *Rhetorical Treatises*. Loeb Classical Library. Cambridge: Harvard University Press, 1939–54.

Hermogenes. See Baldwin, Rabe, and Hock.

Hock, Ronald F., and O'Neil, Edward N. *The Chreia in Ancient Rhetoric. Volume I. The Progymnasmata*. Atlanta: Scholars Press, 1986.

Quintilian. Trans. H. E. Butler. Loeb Classical Library. 4 vols. Cambridge: Harvard University Press, 1920–22.

Rabe, H., ed. *Hermogenis opera*. Rhetores Graeci VI. Lipsiae: Teubner Verlag, 1913.

Rhetorica ad Herennium. Trans. Harry Caplan. Loeb Classical Library (See Cicero, *Rhetoric ad Herennium*). Cambridge: Harvard University Press, 1954.

Theon. See Walz and Butts.

Walz, Christian, ed. *Rhetores Graeci*. 5 vols. Stuttgart: Cottae, 1832–36.

B. MODERN STUDIES OF RHETORIC

Booth, Wayne C.
1961   *The Rhetoric of Fiction*. Chicago: University of Chicago Press. (2nd ed., 1982)

Burke, Kenneth
1969   *A Grammar of Motives*. Berkeley: University of California Press.

1969   *A Rhetoric of Motives*. Berkeley: University of California Press.

1970   *The Rhetoric of Religion. Studies in Logology.* Berkeley: University of California Press.

Clark, Donald L.
1957   *Rhetoric in Greco-Roman Education.* New York: Columbia University Press.

Farenga, Vincent
1979   "Periphrasis on the Origin of Rhetoric." *Modern Language Notes* 94/5, 1033–55.

Kennedy, George A.
1963   *The Art of Persuasion in Greece.* Princeton: Princeton University Press.

1980   *Classical Rhetoric and its Christian and Secular Tradition from Ancient to Modern Times.* Chapel Hill: University of North Carolina Press.

Lausberg, Heinrich
1960   *Handbuch der literarischen Rhetorik.* Munich: Hueber Verlag.

Perelman, Chaim, and Olbrechts-Tyteca, L.
1969   *The New Rhetoric. A Treatise on Argumentation.* Notre Dame, Ind.: University of Notre Dame Press.

C. RHETORICAL CRITICISM OF THE NEW TESTAMENT

Attridge, Harold W.
1988   *The Epistle to the Hebrews.* Hermeneia Commentary. Philadelphia: Fortress Press.

Bauer, Karl Ludwig
1774   *Logica Paullina.* Halae: Impensis Orphanotrophei.

1782   *Rhetorica Paullina.* 2 vols. Halae: Impensis Orphanotrophei.

Betz, Hans-Dieter
1975   "The Literary Composition and Function of Paul's Letter to the Galatians." *New Testament Studies* 21, 353–79.

1979   *Galatians: A Commentary of Paul's Letter to the Churches in Galatia.* Hermeneia Commentary. Philadelphia: Fortress Press.

1985   *2 Corinthians 8 and 9: A Commentary on Two Administrative Letters of the Apostle Paul.* Hermeneia Commentary. Philadelphia: Fortress Press.

1986   "The Problem of Rhetoric and Theology according to the Apostle Paul." In *L'Apôtre Paul. personalitè, style et concêption du Ministère*, ed. A. Vanhoye, Bibliotheca ephemeridum theologicarum lovaniensium 73, 16–48. Leuven: Leuven University Press.

Black, C. Clifton II
1988   "The Rhetorical Form of the Hellenistic Jewish and Early Christian Sermon: A Response to Lawrence Wills," *Harvard Theological Review* 81/1, 1–18.

Blumauer, Karl
1979   "Kriterien wahren und falschen Glaubens. Eine Untersuchung zur paulinischen Argumentation." Th.D. diss., University of Innsbruck.

Brinsmead, Bernard H.
1982   *Galatians. Dialogical Response to Opponents.* Society of Biblical Literature Dissertation Series 65. Atlanta: Scholars Press.

Buenker, Michael
1984   *Briefformular und rhetorische Disposition im 1. Korintherbrief.* Göttingen: Vandenhoeck & Ruprecht.

Bujard, W.
1973   *Stilanalytische Untersuchungen zum Kolosserbrief.* Studien zur Umwelt des Neuen Testaments 11. Göttingen: Vandenhoeck & Ruprecht.

Bultmann, Rudolf
1910   *Der Stil der paulinischen Predigt und die stoisch-kynische Diatribe.* Forschungen zur Religion und Literatur des Alten und Neuen Testaments 13. Göttingen: Vandenhoeck & Ruprecht.

Butts, James R.
1983   "Jesus and the Fox: Paradigm for Pronouncement(s) of Jesus." Unpublished seminar paper, Claremont Graduate School.

Cameron, Ron
1988   " 'What Have You Come Out To See?': Characterizations of John and Jesus in the Gospels." Seminar Paper, Society of Biblical Literature. (Forthcoming in *Semeia*)

Castelli, Elizabeth
1987   "Mimesis as a Discourse of Power in Paul's Letters." Ph.D. diss., Claremont Graduate School.

Church, F. Forrester
1978   "Rhetorical Structure and Design in Paul's Letter to Phi-
             lemon." *Harvard Theological Review* 7/1–2, 17–33.
DuToit, A. B.
1985   "Hyperbolic Contrasts: A Neglected Aspect of Paul's
             Style." Colloquium Biblicum Lovaniense 73. Leuven:
             Leuven University Press.
Forbes, Christopher
1986   "Paul's Boasting and Hellenistic Rhetoric." *New Testa-
             ment Studies* 32, 1–30.
Hanson, A. T.
1974   *Studies in Paul's Technique and Theology.* London:
             SPCK; Grand Rapids: Wm. B. Eerdmans.
Heinrici, Carl F. G.
1887   *Das zweite Sendschreiben des Apostels Paulus an die
             Korinther.* Berlin: Hertz.
Hester, James D.
1984   "The Rhetorical Structure of Galatians 1:11—2:14." *Jour-
             nal of Biblical Literature* 103/2, 223–33.
1986   "The Use and Influence of Rhetoric in Galatians 2:1–14."
             Theologische Zeitschrift 42, 386–408.
Huebner, Hans
1984   "Der Galaterbrief und das Verhältnis von antiker Rhe-
             torik und Epistolographie." *Theologische Literaturzei-
             tung* 109/4, 241–50.
Hughes, Frank W.
1984   "Second Thessalonians as a Document of Early Christian
             Rhetoric." Ph.D. diss. Garrett-Northwestern University.
Jewett, Robert
1982   "Romans as an Ambassadorial Letter." *Interpretation* 36,
             5–20.
1987   *The Thessalonian Correspondence: Pauline Rhetoric and
             Millenarian Piety.* Philadelphia: Fortress Press.
Johanson, Bruce C.
1987   *To All the Brethren: A Text-Linguistic and Rhetorical
             Approach to 1 Thessalonians.* Coniectanea Biblica 16.
             Stockholm: Almquist & Wiksell International.
Kemmler, Dieter Werner
1975   *Faith and Human Reason: A Study of Paul's Method of
             Preaching as Illustrated by 1–2 Thessalonians and Acts
             17:2–4.* Novum Testamentum, Suppl. 40. Leiden: E. J.
             Brill.

Kennedy, George A.
1984   *New Testament Interpretation through Rhetorical Criticism.* Chapel Hill: University of North Carolina Press.

Kinneavy, James L.
1987   *Greek Rhetorical Origins of Christian Faith.* New York: Oxford University Press.

Kraftchick, Steven J.
1985   *Ethos and Pathos in Galatians Five and Six: A Rhetorical Analysis.* Ph.D. diss., Emory University.

Mack, Burton L.
1984   "Decoding the Scripture: Philo and the Rules of Rhetoric." In *Nourished with Peace: Studies in Hellenistic Judaism in Memory of Samuel Sandmel,* ed. F. E. Greenspahn, E. Hilgert, and B. L. Mack, 81–115. Chico, Calif.: Scholars Press.
1987   *Anecdotes and Arguments: The Chreia in Antiquity and Early Christianity.* Occasional Papers 10. Claremont, Calif.: Institute for Antiquity and Christianity.
1988   *A Myth of Innocence: Mark and Christian Origins.* Philadelphia: Fortress Press.
1988   "The Kingdom That Didn't Come: A Social History of the Q Tradents." Society of Biblical Literature Seminar Papers. Atlanta: Scholars Press, 1989.

Mack, Burton L. and Robbins, Vernon K.
1989   *Patterns of Persuasion in the Gospels.* Sonoma, Calif.: Polebridge Press.

Muilenburg, James
1969   "Form Criticism and Beyond." *Journal of Biblical Literature* 88/1, 1–18.

Parrott, Rod
1985   "Rhetoric in the Sociology of Conflict: An Examination of Mark 2:23–28." Society of Biblical Literature Seminar Paper.

Petersen, Norman R.
1985   *Rediscovering Paul: Philemon and the Sociology of Paul's Narrative World.* Philadelphia: Fortress Press.

Reedy, Charles J.
1983   "Greco-Roman Rhetorical Influence on Matthean Pronouncement Stories." Unpublished Paper presented to the Great Lakes Region, Society of Biblical Literature/ Catholic Biblical Association.

Robbins, Vernon K.
1983   "Pronouncement Stories and Jesus' Blessing of the Chil-
            dren: A Rhetorical Approach." *Semeia* 29, 43–74.
1984   *Jesus the Teacher. A Socio-rhetorical Interpretation of
            Mark.* Philadelphia: Fortress Press.
1985   "Picking Up the Fragments: From Crossan's Analysis to
            Rhetorical Analysis." *Foundations and Facets Forum* 1/
            2, 31–64.
1987   "Pronouncement Stories from a Rhetorical Perspective."
            Society of Biblical Literature Seminar Paper.

Schneider, Norbert
1970   *Die rhetorische Eigenart der paulinischen Antithese.*
            Hermeneutische Untersuchungen zur Theologie 11.
            Tübingen: J. C. B. Mohr (Paul Siebeck).

Schüssler Fiorenza, Elizabeth
1988   "The Ethics of Interpretation: Decentering Biblical
            Scholarship." *Journal of Biblical Literature* 107/1, 3–17.

Scroggs, Robins
1976   "Paul as Rhetorician: Two Homilies in Romans 1–11." In
            Jews, Greeks, and Christians, essays in honor of W. D.
            Davies, ed. R. Hamerton-Kelly and R. Scroggs, 271–
            320. Leiden: E. J. Brill.

Shaw, Graham
1983   *The Cost of Authority: Manipulation and Freedom in the
            New Testament.* London: SCM Press.

Siegert, Folker
1985   *Argumentation bei Paulus gezeigt an Römer 9 bis 11.*
            Tübingen: J. C. B. Mohr (Paul Siebeck).

Silva, Moises
1980   "The Pauline Style as Lexical Choice: Ginoskein and
            Related Verbs." In *Pauline Studies,* in honor of F. F.
            Bruce, 184–207. Grand Rapids: Wm. B. Eerdmans.

Smiga, G.
1985   "Language, Experience, and Theology: The Argumen-
            tation of Galatians 3:6—4:7 in Light of the Literary Form
            of the Letter." Th.D. diss., Pontifica Universitas Gre-
            goriana.

Staley, Jeffrey L.
1988   *The Print's First Kiss: A Rhetorical Investigation of the
            Implied Reader in the Fourth Gospel.* Society of Biblical
            Literature Dissertation Series 82. Atlanta: Scholars
            Press.

Standaert, Beno
1983   "Analyse rhetorique des chapitres 12 a 14 de 1 Co." In *Charisma und Agape*, ed. Lorenzo de Lorenzi, 23–50. Rome: Abbey of St. Paul-Outside-the-Wall.
1986   "La rhetorique ancienne dans saint Paul." In *L'Apôtre Paul: personalitè, style et concêption du ministère*, ed. A. Vanhoye, Bibliotheca ephemeridum theologicarum lovaniensium 73; 78–92. Leuven: Leuven University Press.

Stowers, Stanley K.
1981   *The Diatribe and Paul's Letter to the Romans.* Society of Biblical Literature Dissertation Series 57. Missoula, Mont.: Scholars Press.
1984   "Social Status, Public Speaking and Private Teaching: The Circumstances of Paul's Preaching Activity." *Novum Testamentum* 26/1, 59–82.

Watson, Duane F.
1984   "Rhetorical Criticism and Its Implications for the Question of the Unity of Philippians." Unpublished paper presented at the Society of Biblical Literature.

Weiss, Johannes
1897   "Beiträge zur paulinischen Rhetorik." In *Theologische Studien*, Bernhard Weiss zu seinem 70, Geburtstag dargebracht, 165–247. Göttingen: Vandenhoeck & Ruprecht.

Wendand, Hans
1924   *Der zweite Korintherbrief.* Meyer Kommentar 6. Göttingen: Vandenhoeck & Ruprecht. (Reprinted 1970)

Wilder, Amos N.
1964   *Early Christian Rhetoric: The Language of the Gospel.* New York: Harper & Row. (Reprint, Cambridge: Harvard University Press, 1971)

Wilke, Christian G.
1843   *Die neutestamentliche Rhetorik: Ein Seitenstuck zur Grammatik des neutestamentlichen Sprachidioms.* Dresden/Leipzig: Arnold.

Wills, Lawrence
1984   "The Form of the Sermon in Hellenistic Judaism and Early Christianity." *Harvard Theological Review* 77, 277–99.

Wonneberger, R.

1976   "Ansätze zu einer textlinquistischen Beschreibung der Argumentation bei Paulus." In *Textlinquistik und Semantik*, ed. Meid and Keller. Innsbrucker Beiträge zur Sprachwissenshaft 17, 159–78. Innsbruck: The University Press.

Wuellner, Wilhelm

1976   "Paul's Rhetoric of Argumentation in Romans." *Catholic Biblical Quarterly* 38, 330–51. (Reprint, *The Romans Debate*, ed. Karl Donfried, 152–74. Minneapolis: Augsburg Publishing House, 1977).

1978   "Toposforschung und Torah Interpretation bei Paulus und Jesus." *New Testament Studies* 24, 463–83.

1979   "Greek Rhetoric and Pauline Argumentation." In *Early Christian Literature and the Classical Tradition*, in honorem Robert M. Grant, ed. William R. Schoedel and Robert L. Wilken, 177–88. Paris: Editions Beauchesne.

1986   "Paul as Pastor: The Function of Rhetorical Questions in First Corinthians." *In L'Apôtre Paul: personalitè, style et concêption du ministère*, ed. A. Vanhoye, Bibliotheca ephemeridum theologicarum lovaniensium 73, 49–77. Leuven: Leuven University Press.

1987   "Where is Rhetorical Criticism Taking Us?" *Catholic Biblical Quarterly* 49/3, 448–63.